D1577704

HARD TIMES
AND *Holy Places*

HARD TIMES
AND *Holy Places*

KRISTIN WARNER BELCHER

DESERET
BOOK

SALT LAKE CITY, UTAH

Library of Congress Cataloging-in-Publication Data

Belcher, Kristin Warner.
   Hard times and holy places / Kristin Warner Belcher.
      p. cm.
   Summary: A rare form of cancer caused the author to lose the sight in one eye in her childhood. Another cancer in her adulthood (the result of radiation from the earlier cancer treatments) left her totally blind. Her journey of the spirit to find holy places in the midst of her hard times is the focus of this book.
   ISBN 978-1-60641-051-6 (hardbound : alk. paper)
   1. Suffering—Religious aspects—Christianity.   2. Hope—Religious aspects—Christianity.   3. Cancer—Patients—Biography.   I. Title.
   BV4909.B45 2009
   248.8'6092—dc22
   [B]   2008053666

Printed in the United States of America
Publishers Printing, Salt Lake City, UT

10   9   8   7   6   5   4   3   2   1

To my mother, Susan Pinney Warner

Mom, you have dreamed of writing a book—
consider it done. So many of the truths I have shared
in these pages, I learned from you.

Contents

INTRODUCTION

One of my lofty childhood dreams was to lead a parade as a talented majorette, prancing along in a sparkling costume. I would dazzle thousands as I performed astounding tricks with my baton, and when the crowd saw me throw it high into the air, they would oooh and ahhh at my incredible skill, grace, and dexterity. It would be an event never to be forgotten.

There were some slight problems with my plan. I didn't own a baton, I didn't really know how to twirl one, and I couldn't see well enough to catch a baton if I threw it too high above me. But nothing could hinder my dream. I begged my mother to give me a baton for Christmas, and then I waited for the gift that would make me famous.

My mother did purchase my dream baton—and then

she hid it in a safe place where I wouldn't find it. Unfortunately, when Christmas arrived, Mom couldn't remember where the "special place" was.

Although I was disappointed at not receiving my key to stardom, this experience provided plenty of fodder with which to tease my mother over the years. When anything came up missing, I'd say, "It's probably with my baton." It was inconceivable to me how Mom could forget where she had put something, especially something as vital to my life as my baton.

Now that I am a busy mother, I completely understand the disappearing object phenomenon. Most everything in my home has its own place, but occasionally I need to hide something from my children. Like my mother, I stash things in "special places," and it baffles me when I can't remember where they are. Perhaps there is a black hole in my home . . . or is it in my memory?

To avoid the ravenous black hole, I often shove things into my "junk drawer." I can rummage through this drawer if I happen to need the item; otherwise I just forget about it. It is nice to have a spot to throw the odds and ends into, and then just shut the drawer.

Perhaps you are like me and wish you had a "junk

drawer" into which you could shove problems and trials when you don't want or aren't quite sure how to handle them. Or maybe, emotionally, you might wish for adversity to be swallowed up and disappear in some "special place," like my baton did. It would be so much easier to stash away difficulties and not have to struggle through the pain. But there isn't a "junk drawer" large enough to store all the hardships you and I face in mortality.

At a very young age, I learned that my problems weren't going to disappear; they were real and couldn't be escaped or ignored. Still, I wished for it to be otherwise.

Throughout my life, I have dealt with a myriad of physical problems that have overwhelmed and taxed me to my very limit. However, nothing I have experienced can compare to the life-threatening situation I found myself engulfed in five years ago. Boy, did I wish my trials would just vanish!

Five major surgeries within the space of five months left me physically and emotionally devastated. I had never experienced anything this tragic. It seemed the misery and trauma would never have an end.

The months following the surgeries were horrendous.

I had fought to save my life, yet I didn't want to live like this.

Now that I am five years removed from the initial trauma, I am able to look back and recognize the Lord's loving hand throughout the whole experience. I see that He heard my literal cries for help, courage, and comfort. I see that He guided me in the many difficult decisions I had to make. I can see that He sent me to a loving family who cared and served unceasingly for me. I can see that He sent members of my ward to me who served as angels with true charity. I see that I grew closer to my husband and that together we grew closer to Christ and to the Father.

This was a horrible and devastating time in my life, yet it was also spotted with times of holiness and spiritual strengthening. I do not wish to go through the entire trauma and pain again; however, I am grateful to have had those times of holiness. I now think of those moments as my "holy places."

Normally, when I hear the commandment to "stand ye in holy places" (D&C 87:8), I think of being in the temple or at church. When I am feeling discouraged or overwhelmed with the pressures of life, I love to be surrounded with calmness within the walls of the temple. There is something wonderful about worshiping in God's holy house that brings peace to my heart and puts troubles into their proper perspective. I can feel the holiness of the building when I enter the temple doors and am, for a little while, separated from the world. It is a heavenly retreat of order in a world of confusion and turmoil.

Oh, how I wish I could remain within the protective walls of the temple, but I can't live there. I realize that it is my time to live in the world and to struggle with the difficulties of mortality. Even when my spirit longs to be with the Father and away from trials and troubles, I know that it is my time of mortal proving. But I am grateful that I can recharge my spiritual strength by worshiping the Father in His holy temple.

The chapel of my own local church building is also a place of holiness for my spirit. Here, I go to partake of the holy sacrament and renew my sacred covenants with my Heavenly Father. I love to sing the hymns with my friends in the congregation and long each week to be filled with the doctrine of Christ. Like the temple, the chapel is a holy place to go to worship and renew strength for the battles of mortal life. But it is not a holy place in which to reside.

I am coming to realize that everyday life offers many

opportunities for me to "stand in holy places" even when I am not in church, at the temple, or in other places I typically think of as holy. Trials and difficulties can, if we let them, become holy places—places where we can commune with the Father through the Spirit, places where we can feel the power of the Atonement in our lives. Our personal hard times can become our personal holy places. Such holy places will, through the power of Christ, provide purifying and refining for our souls. Our struggles can be consecrated to our good and growth, and you and I can become more like Christ. The challenges we might have banished to the "junk drawer" can bless us in mortality and throughout eternity.

It is my hope that, as I share my story, you will pray continually. Pray that the Spirit will teach you, comfort you, encourage you, and direct you. As you read, I invite you to think of the hardships you are currently facing in your life. I know that the Father will guide your heart to the help you need. Your hard times can become, as mine have, your own personal holy places in which to stand.

Chapter One

THE FOUNDATION OF HOLY PLACES

Christ is the solid foundation on which to build holy places. Without Him and His power, hard times are simply that—hard times. The best we can do is just hope to get through them. We will struggle and flail and long for their end, but we will not be enduring well, conquering the trials, or mastering ourselves. In order to turn our hard times into holy times, we must first rely on Jesus Christ.

When I was an infant, my parents demonstrated their reliance on the Savior as they followed heaven's promptings on my behalf. Although I was too young to remember the actual experience, the inspiration they received stands as a true holy place in my life.

When I was seven months old, at a well-check visit with our pediatrician, my mother was given some heartbreaking news. The doctor examined my eyes and found something terribly wrong. Mom was sent to our family ophthalmologist for an additional exam, and I was diagnosed with bilateral retinoblastoma. This meant I had multiple tumors on the retinas of both eyes—a childhood cancer that was nearly always fatal. My parents were understandably devastated with this news, and my mother even planned my funeral.

Putting their trust in Heavenly Father, my parents visited yet another doctor. This renowned specialist examined my eyes and announced that the next day I would have my right eye, the worst of the two, removed. The other eye would be treated with radiation. This was one school of thought for the treatment of retinoblastoma. In shock, my parents stated their desire for a second opinion. They felt a sense of darkness and unease with this treatment approach. They didn't feel right about this doctor or his proposed plan of action.

My parents fasted, prayed, and counseled with their bishop. With help from the Lord, they were led to another doctor at Stanford University Medical Center, about an hour and a half away from our home.

After my eye examination, the doctor presented his treatment plan. Hoping to preserve sight in both eyes, he proposed that both be radiated. My mother and father felt totally different when given this plan than with the first approach. They knew this treatment option was the right course to take. The Spirit confirmed their feelings and they went forward with the treatment.

Under general anesthesia, I was put into a large machine. The radiation beams were aimed at the identifying marks placed on each of my temples, and the process began. Over the course of several months, my eyes, including all the bones and tissues surrounding them, were blasted with radiation in the hope that I would live. When the radiation course was complete, the cancer was eradicated! Miraculously, my life had been preserved, the tumors had been destroyed, and some of my vision in both eyes had been saved.

This would be a fantastic ending to the story; however, God's great wisdom and comprehension of all things was to be made manifest even further. About eight years later, I lost the sight in my left eye. I was left with only limited vision in my right. If my parents had followed the insistent specialist with the first approach, my right eye would have been removed and I would have been completely blind when I was eight years old.

God knew more than my parents, and He knew more than the specialist. As my parents turned to the Lord and relied on His promptings, He directed my mother and father in what was best for me in each crucial moment, as well as for my future. I am incredibly grateful for the promptings my parents were given and for their obedience in following the direction of the Lord. Not only was my life saved, but I was able to see for more than thirty-two years.

This critical time in the early months of my life is a continual reminder to me of the wisdom of God. It remains a holy place in my heart. It is holy because of Jesus Christ—His direction, His protection, and His encircling love.

Relying on Christ requires correct knowledge of His characteristics and attributes, which will ultimately lead us to know Him.

As a young teenage girl, I had an experience with the Spirit that strengthened my knowledge and understanding of Jesus Christ. I had always had a close relationship with my Savior, yet He became more real as I learned of His character. What started out as a negative experience has become another holy place in my heart.

Through the car window, I watched the water below as

my mother and I crossed the San Francisco Bay Bridge. We were returning from a routine eye checkup, and Mom, having a captive audience, began teaching me what she had learned from Joseph Smith's *Lectures on Faith*. I was not in the mood for Church stuff, and I let my irritation show. However, my display of annoyance did not deter Mom. She kept right on talking about the attributes possessed by the Lord. I'm not sure when, but somewhere over the Bay my heart softened and my spirit was receptive to truth—truth that I would depend on fiercely in the future.

Mother recited the characteristics of Christ, and I would try to repeat the list without forgetting any. We took turns until both of us had mastered the list. We discussed each characteristic, and I began to value their meanings more deeply. I still remember the sense of accomplishment and enlightenment that replaced my annoyance.

I learned that God was God before and after the creation of the world. He is merciful, gracious, slow to anger, and abundant in goodness. God changes not; He is a God of truth and cannot lie—not that He doesn't lie, but that He *cannot* lie. That is His character. Also, God is no respecter of persons, and finally, God is love (*Lectures on Faith* [Salt Lake City: Deseret Book, 1985], 3:9–26). Christ is like His Father in the possession of these characteristics. If I learn His character and come to know Him, I am coming to know the Father as well.

Additionally, the knowledge of God's attributes promotes the exercise of my faith. These attributes include: knowledge, faith or power, justice, judgment, mercy, and truth (*Lectures on Faith*, 4:4–19).

I had learned these attributes before, but that day on the Bay Bridge, the Spirit burned them into my heart. I desired more than ever to develop these same traits.

That day, the Bay Bridge became a holy place. When I think of that bridge, I will always remember my mother teaching me truth, even when I didn't want to hear it. I will remember my change of heart and the teaching power of the Holy Ghost. That experience strengthened my love for my Savior. Time after time, I have leaned on these attributes when life has become difficult. Because I know that Christ does not change, I know I can and will continue to depend on Him in future difficulties. I am extremely grateful for that unlikely classroom—my holy place.

Since that trip over the Bay Bridge, I have been eager to learn all I can about Jesus Christ. To aid me in my quest, I purchased an inexpensive copy of the Book of Mormon for my study. Inside the front cover, I wrote, "What are the characteristics, attributes, and titles of Christ?" This time as I studied the Book of Mormon, I highlighted only the attributes and titles of Christ, listing each under my question in the front. I was excited to see how much this book of scripture revealed about the Savior. His characteristics and attributes are revealed everywhere. I truly came to know Him better. Additionally, I realized how well the ancient prophets knew Him. Through this exercise, my love for and testimony of Christ has grown. I know He is the Son of God.

I have found verses about Christ in the scriptures that have taught me, comforted me, and given me hope and courage. One verse that teaches me about Christ's nature is Mosiah 4:9: "Believe in God; believe that he is, and that he created all things, both in heaven and in earth; believe that he has all wisdom, and all power, both in heaven and in earth; believe that man doth not comprehend all the things which the Lord can comprehend."

I love those words of King Benjamin, in which he urged his people, as well as me and you, to believe that God "is." Not just that He was, but that He *is*. I know that He is alive and present in our lives today. He loves you and

He loves me. He knows perfectly our sorrows and sadness, our pain and heartache, and our hopes and joys.

The last line of this verse teaches me that God comprehends more than I do. He has the whole plan in mind and knows how my difficulties can help me become like Him. Even when I think I know what is best, His wisdom and knowledge far surpass my understanding.

On the Bay Bridge, so many years ago, there was much more going on than I realized. My mother taught me knowledge from her mind, but, more importantly, she taught me what she knew in her heart. When I was an infant, she had experienced firsthand many of the attributes of Christ. Mother had come to know Him more deeply as she struggled through the traumatic months of diagnosis and treatment for my cancer. The Bay Bridge, my holy place, spanned more than just water that day. It connected two minds in the knowledge and truth of Christ and two hearts through the Spirit in love.

Chapter Two

CHOOSING CHRIST

Perhaps Santa Claus never got my Christmas list that year, or maybe the elf reading my letter was in the lower reading group. Whatever the reason, Santa did not deliver the right gift. Rabbit fur coats were "in" when I was in sixth grade, and I wanted one so badly. I knew that old Saint Nick would leave a soft fur coat under the Christmas tree just for me. The beautiful fur would feel so wonderful beneath my fingers, and I would look beautiful wrapped in its warmth. The closer it got to Christmas, the closer I was to my rabbit fur coat. I just knew it!

I had an expectation, but that year it did not match reality. Santa did bring me a fur coat, but it wasn't rabbit, and it wasn't real fur. My brothers and sisters called it my "possum coat." It was neither soft nor beautiful. In fact, it was a kind of wiry fake fur. I was so disappointed.

Many times in life, our expectations are very different from what really happens. That fact can produce frustration, disappointment, sorrow, and heartache. Whether our expectations are large or small, important or unimportant, whether we formed them as children or as adults, we want them to come true. Maybe it comes from watching too many animated fairy-tale movies, but it seems like we expect happy endings—happily ever afters—which seldom come. However, it is Satan, not Walt Disney, who wants us to feel upset and angry at the unfairness of reality. Instead of trouble-free bliss, we face trials and challenges, difficulties that we feel we don't deserve and that get in the way of our plans.

No one schedules adversity. We don't look at our daily planners and say, "Today I'll drop off the kids at school, go grocery shopping, get a fatal disease, pick up the dry cleaning, have marital problems, and take dinner to Sister So-and-so. If I have time, maybe I can lose my job and my house could burn down. Or should I push that off until tomorrow?" In this mortal world, we have no need to schedule trials; they just come.

So when we are disappointed because "it wasn't supposed to happen like this," or "everything was going so right until this happened," what do we do?

I had another expectation for my life that was much more serious than receiving a rabbit fur coat. In my young mind, I expected that, at some point, things would change and I would be able to see and look like everyone around me. When I realized this would not be my reality, I was absolutely crushed.

The radiation treatment I underwent as an infant killed the cancer, but it also damaged all the bones and tissues around my eyes. As my face grew, my eyes and the area around them did not. My hourglass-shaped face caused me to look different from other children, and I began to notice the stares of others. I couldn't do all the things that I wanted to because of my sight and doctor's restrictions, and I felt frustrated. However, somehow I thought this would eventually change, and I waited for that change to occur.

My parents were very good to explain things to me a little at a time as I grew older and could make sense of it all. Yet something didn't click until one unforgettable day.

My mother and I had traveled to the eye clinic for yet

another checkup. While I sat in the exam chair, it hit me. I didn't know what the doctor and my mother were discussing, but it didn't matter. In my head I had realized that this was as good as it was going to get. I would never see any better. This was permanent, and I would have to live my life with this problem. Like it or not, this was my reality. But that was not what I had planned for my life!

I was silent through the rest of the exam, but when we left the room, I began to sob. I wept out loud and grew scared and angry. There in the hallway of the medical center, I threw a royal tantrum. Thoughts of how it wasn't fair filled my mind. This wasn't what I wanted.

As my storm of emotion raged, my mother sat me down on a bench and held me in her arms. She allowed me to cry while she prayed for guidance. The Spirit blessed her with the words to calm me. She sweetly explained that I had a choice to make. Either I could be angry, bitter, and upset, like I was then doing, or I could pray to Heavenly Father and ask Him for help. I could tell Him how scared I was and allow Him to comfort me. Mom told me that Heavenly Father loved me and would help me get through this.

After a few minutes I stopped crying, took my mother's hand, and began the trip home. When we arrived, I went to my room. Some time later, I found my mom in the kitchen and told her I had prayed. I had poured out my fears to Heavenly Father and asked Him to help me. I had received a literal answer. Jesus had promised me He would stay with me and give me the help I needed when life was hard.

Discovering that the expectations I had held onto would never come true was devastating. But through this experience I gained vital understanding from my mother and from Christ. I had a choice. Right there in the medical center hallway, I made a conscious choice to turn to Christ rather than to remain angry and bitter. That hallway became a holy place for me.

Also, I found that through praying to my Father in Heaven, I could receive direct answers in the very moment I needed them. The reality was that Jesus Christ would be with me through the difficult times ahead.

When hardships come, I try to remember what I learned that day in that holy place. When I have turned to Christ, I have always received help to make it through. But sometimes life gets a little unbearable, and we want to run away from our difficulties. I have felt this so many times.

Although I had an absolutely loving family and wonderful childhood, my young mind didn't always comprehend this. When I was growing up, Cinderella was a character with whom I could definitely relate. I felt like I had to do all the work in my home and was sure that if we had had a cellar, I would have had to sleep down there. The fact that I had two sisters was further evidence that I was living a Cinderella syndrome. It was not fair!

I would often pack my small flowered suitcase and make my way to a place where I wouldn't have to clean my room or do the "poop scoop." There I would be appreciated, loved, and given cookies. The home of a sweet couple, whom I called Aunt Barbara and Uncle Joe, was my destination and safe haven. But each time I would begin my trek, one of my parents would always pick me up. I never made it the whole way. I always had to go right back and finish my chores.

I found out quickly that running away was not the answer. It is an option, but not the solution to problems. Sometimes it only compounds the trouble. To this day, when I am frustrated with some difficulty, my sisters will tease, "Why don't you go pack your little floral suitcase and run away to Aunt Barbara's?" It has become a standing joke between us.

When hard times come, we have several options. We can become angry and bitter, try to run away, or turn to the Father and ask for help. Our natural tendency may be to throw a tantrum and get mad when reality does not match our expectations. But that is not the Savior's way. He willingly suffered so He would know how to help us. When faced with tribulation, whether large or small, we can make the choice to turn to Him. When we do, we will find ourselves in a position to receive His assistance and strength to endure well. He will help us conquer the challenges we face.

After the wars temporarily concluded in the Book of Alma, we see how the people were affected. Some chose to turn away from Christ, while others humbled themselves and turned toward Him. In Alma 62:41 we learn, "But behold, because of the exceedingly great length of the war between the Nephites and the Lamanites many had become hardened, because of the exceedingly great length of the war; and many were softened because of their afflictions, insomuch that they did humble themselves before God, even in the depth of humility."

Like the Nephites, we can choose to harden or soften our hearts when challenging times come. Choosing to turn to Christ may not be easy at first, but it will ultimately lead us back to Him. It is really the only way to do more than just struggle. With His power we can overcome.

Once we have made the choice to turn to Christ during trials, there is real work to do in order for our hard times to become holy places. We learn about this in 2 Nephi 32:9: "But behold, I say unto you that ye must pray always, and not faint; that ye must not perform any thing unto the Lord save in the first place ye shall pray unto the Father in the name of Christ, that he will consecrate thy performance unto thee, that thy performance may be for the welfare of thy soul."

I want my suffering and struggling to mean something for my benefit. I know there will be trials for me to endure, but I want them to strengthen and improve me, not just flatten me. Nephi gives us the key to make this happen. When I pray continually to the Father before I do anything, He can and will consecrate those things for the welfare of my soul. I consecrate myself to Him, and He consecrates all I do for my good. This makes the struggle worth something marvelous.

I have put this to the test. On those days when I didn't have any idea how I could go on, I have prayed and asked Father to help me and to consecrate the pain for my good. Looking back, I see that help did come, and I have grown stronger. The Father sees more than I do how I have been blessed through the process of consecration. Each trial I offer to Him has been consecrated for my welfare and good.

Whatever the problem, whatever pain you are experiencing, I invite you to try an experiment. Pray and consecrate all you do to the Father. See how He consecrates those actions to your benefit. I know it works. Don't allow your heart to be hardened by hard times; make the choice to turn to Christ and those hard times will become holy.

Chapter Three

TRUSTING THE SAVIOR

In my early teenage years, my family traveled from California to Utah for a vacation at a camp in Provo Canyon. During this trip, my father took my two younger brothers and me on a hike up the northeast face of Mount Timpanogos. He was told there was a paved path, and he expected it to be an enjoyable but not too challenging hike for his novice climbers. At the trailhead, we were excited to begin the climb, but soon found some major obstacles in our way.

Although it was the middle of July, the mountain face along with our path was covered with slick ice and snow. I wore only thin tennis shoes with no treads on the bottom, providing me no traction, and I slid all over the place. My limited vision and poor depth perception added to a treacherous journey. Our ice-blanketed path ran next to a dangerous dropoff and, although I wouldn't admit it, I was in trouble.

My father had been prompted to grab a rope from the car as we left, and, much to my chagrin, he tied one end around my waist and one end around his, with about three feet of slack between us. Dad explained that, with the rope, he could keep me safe and prevent my falling over the edge. Well, I was a "cool" teenager, and this was beyond humiliating. I'm sure we provided entertainment for the other hikers, but I was not amused. At first I protested the arrangement; however, Dad said we had only two choices: we could climb tied together or return to the car. I resigned myself to complete humiliation and began the slippery trek upward.

While my little brothers climbed carefree all around the ice mountain, I shifted from embarrassment to annoyance. They were just little kids, and here I was lashed to Dad. It wasn't fair. I could do it on my own and wished my father would realize it. Determined to prove it, I hiked on my own and tried to ignore the rope connection to Dad. Soon, however, my attitude changed. Several times, I came close to sliding off the edge. My fall was prevented only by my father's quick reaction and watchful care. He pulled the rope tight, and I was safe. I stopped complaining and tried to watch my step. While looking down, I noticed my father's large footprints in the snow. If I placed each foot directly into his footprints, I would be safe. I took care to follow his trail exactly and only rarely did I slide enough to warrant his help. Instead of being angry or annoyed with Dad, I let go of my pride and trusted him. I knew that if he stepped in a particular place, I could safely step there as well. In this way, we made our way up the difficult terrain.

When we stopped to eat our sack lunch, I looked at the beautiful vista below and marveled at how far I had climbed. I knew I wouldn't have been able to make it by myself and, finally, felt grateful for Dad and the rope. The climb was taxing, but worth it.

Due to the large amounts of snow and ice, the top of the trail was closed to hikers. We were disappointed not to be permitted to the top, but felt we had conquered the mountain anyway.

The descent was even more dangerous than the climb. I trusted Dad's direction and again stepped in his footprints. I knew he was there to protect me, and Dad kept me safe from harm. Sure, I fell down a lot, and the seat of my jeans was soaked from slipping onto my backside, but I had done it! Actually, *we* had done it. Dad and I had made the climb together.

This experience has stayed with me through many years, and the principle of trust has become part of me. The icy trek up Mount Timpanogos is another of my holy places. Here I learned to more deeply trust and depend on my father.

Even though I was young, I didn't miss the parallel to mortal life. I know if I anchor myself to Christ, I will be led back to my Father in Heaven. I can follow His footsteps and be spiritually safe on my journey. I fall quite frequently, but my Savior's power has lifted me. His loving and tender care keeps me stepping forward on my path. I trust Him, and we are making the climb together.

Having trust in Jesus Christ is another crucial key in the process of finding holiness amid hardship—trust in His wisdom, trust in His atonement, and trust in His love. Complete understanding is not required; however, waiting on the Lord and exercising faith in Him are absolutely necessary.

My life has been composed of endless opportunities to turn to the Savior in trust and faith. As rapid-fire difficulties have hit me, I have tried to remember to trust my Savior. However, when I find myself submerged in tribulation, my trust in Christ often gives way to doubts and fear. At times, I feel like I did on that difficult mountain trek. But when I leave my anger, discouragement, fear, annoyance, and pride at the feet of Jesus, I see that the trial is an opportunity to learn, more deeply, how to trust Him fully.

So many times, I have relied on the promise found in Alma 36:3. The words Alma gave to his son Helaman give me courage. He said, "Whosoever shall put their trust in God shall be supported in their trials, and their troubles, and their afflictions, and shall be lifted up at the last day."

In this verse, Alma doesn't promise his son that if he places his trust in Christ, he will be free from trials. Instead, he promises that Helaman's trust will secure him support during hard times, as well as the opportunity to dwell with the Lord eternally.

This promise holds true for you and me. Placing our trust in Jesus Christ qualifies us for His support. I absolutely know this is true. Christ has supported and lifted me through so many seemingly unbearable trials and troubles.

One such experience occurred my senior year of high school. Because my face looked different from other people's, I was made fun of and stared at a lot. Due to the reactions of others, it got to the point where I didn't want to go out in public anymore.

I remember being in the mall and watching a man practically fall over himself as he stared at me. Though not in the manner I wanted, I definitely had a face that turned heads. Most of my life I had dealt good-naturedly with the staring and even thought it would be fun to have a T-shirt printed with the statement, "I can see you staring at me." But it got harder and harder to smile about it. It was difficult, as a teenager, not to be pretty but to be a curiosity.

Years earlier, I had been told by my doctors that when I was finished growing in my late teenage years I could have reconstructive surgery to correct my facial abnormality. I didn't want to have surgery; however, my quality of life was being chipped away by stares and rude comments. I had to do something. I began thinking seriously about having the procedure done and prayed for direction in the matter. I received my answer in a general conference address by President Boyd K. Packer.

President Packer spoke of the individuals in the Bible

with disabilities who waited for healing at the waters of Bethesda. His loving words soothed my heart when he said, "I desire to bring comfort to those to whom the words handicapped or disability have very personal meaning" ("The Moving of the Water," *Ensign*, May 1991, 7). Well, I certainly fit in that category, and I felt his words and the Spirit very personally. I prayed for guidance as President Packer taught, and I received my answer through the Spirit when he explained that, for those with disabilities, "Every quarter of an inch of physical and mental improvement is worth striving for" ("The Moving of the Water," 7).

I felt I should move forward with the surgery and do all in my power to improve my situation. The Holy Ghost infused the words of an Apostle into my heart and created another holy place.

Accompanied by my parents, I had an evaluation by a plastic surgeon. He told me, quite rudely, that he would not touch my face surgically until I had my sightless left eye removed and replaced with an artificial eye. Reconstructive surgery would do little to improve my appearance if the eye, discolored from calcification, remained.

I was furious with this man. I was not going to be some

"freak" with a fake eye! The nerve of this guy! What was he thinking? I brooded silently all the way home and would not speak to my parents.

Before we arrived home, my mother presented me with an idea. Mom explained that she knew Heavenly Father had the power to completely heal my unsightly eye, if it were His will to do so. She encouraged me to pray and petition God for healing.

I took this suggestion to heart. I absolutely did not want a prosthetic eye, and prayed to receive God's healing so I wouldn't need the surgery. After I asked for this blessing, my left eye began to burn. It had been hurting for several months, but now the pain was more intense. Each time I prayed for healing, my eye burned more.

I wanted the pain to cease, so I stopped asking for my eye to be healed. I knew I had received my answer. It was not the will of my Heavenly Father to heal my useless eye, although I knew He could. I would need to go through the dreaded experience and live with an artificial eye.

The Holy Ghost taught me that my job was to follow the doctor's recommendation. That answer was difficult to swallow. It was not what I wanted; yet I tried to gather my courage, I placed my trust in Christ, and then I had the surgery.

Emotionally, it was a difficult experience. I wrestled with my feelings and tried to be brave. After healing from the surgery, I was fitted with a prosthetic eye. To my surprise and relief, my confidence grew. I didn't like talking about the fact that my eye was not real, but I knew that accepting the prosthetic eye had been the right thing to do. The pain I had lived with for so long was now completely gone. Although it was not the remedy I had wanted, healing *had* come.

Through Christ, I also felt comfort and peace. It was only with His help that I was able to endure the experience and the emotional ramifications.

A few years later, I had the reconstructive surgery, performed by a different surgeon. This operation took seven hours and was very extensive. Bone and tissue from my own body were grafted in to build up my temples and cheekbones. Other surgical improvements were made, and then the agonizing recovery began.

But complications arose, and fluid began collecting under my scalp. My recovery process came to an abrupt halt. It became necessary for the excess fluid to be drained with a large syringe. Twice a day, my dad, under the direction of my surgeons, stuck a needle into my head and removed large amounts of fluid trapped between my scalp and skull. It was incredibly painful. Each day, it was the same. The problem wasn't getting better, and I was getting worse. The next step of recovery was not attainable until this problem stopped, and it got to the point where I couldn't take it anymore. Both physically and emotionally, I had had enough.

I asked my family to join me as I petitioned Heavenly Father for healing. My father removed a large quantity of fluid while I cried, and then he and my brother-in-law gave me a priesthood blessing. I was promised healing from my current problem. From that moment on, there was no more fluid.

This may seem like a small thing, but for me, it was huge. I had witnessed a miracle in my life. I had trusted in the healing power of Jesus Christ and His priesthood, and had received the needed blessing. I was able to progress in my recovery and had no need of the daily needles. I still had to endure months of physical suffering, but I had been healed amidst the pain.

As my recovery progressed, I trusted that Christ

understood exactly what I was experiencing. No one else could have complete understanding, but Christ could and did. I trusted Him to see me through the remainder of the trial and felt His strength with me.

Unfortunately, over time the surgical improvements to my face faded. The grafted tissue and bone did not have a good enough blood supply, due to my childhood radiation, and the grafts were absorbed by my body. All of that pain would seem wasted, except for that sacred place—a holy place of healing.

Perhaps you are like me, and deal with a disability or other trial that lasts many years. Or maybe your hardships are brief but frequent. No matter the duration or severity of our trials, trusting Christ must become a long-term way of life. Placing our trust in the Savior is one way of always remembering Him, and as we remember Him, we are promised that we may have His Spirit always to be with us (see Moroni 4).

Chapter Four

THE TRUTH ABOUT TRIALS

The next key to turning our hard times into holy places is to understand the purpose of and truth about our trials. Knowing the true doctrine surrounding my challenges has helped me to accept difficulties better and to keep from becoming, or remaining, bitter and angry.

When you have been in the midst of serious difficulties, have you ever wondered, "Why is this happening to me?" or, "Why do I have to suffer like this?" The question "why" seems to come so naturally, but it seldom has an answer, nor does it decrease the stress or pain or take away the trial.

Many years ago, I suffered with a terrible case of mononucleosis. I was down in bed for nearly a year and was in incredible pain. On one of those lovely days, I lay miserable on the couch in the front room of my condo in Provo, Utah. From my vantage point, I had a clear view of the letter "Y," representing Brigham Young University, painted on the mountain outside my window. I remember laughing out loud, saying, "That's a great question: 'Y?' They just forgot the 'WH' part. It should ask, 'WHY?'"

I thought about my current spot of suffering and admitted that there was no room for "whys." They did no good. So I proposed to myself, since I was suggesting changes to the mountain, that they should just add another word to make it say, "WHY NOT?" Why shouldn't this be happening to me?

Replacing our "why" questions with "what" questions will lead us to truth and guide our actions in a more productive direction. We might ask ourselves questions such as:

What can I learn from this difficulty?

What role can this trial play in bringing me closer to Christ?

What can I do to show my faithfulness to my Savior during this struggle?

What can I do to help others who are also suffering?

Finding the answers to those questions will motivate

us to act. We will move past self-pity and closer to Jesus Christ.

Studying the words of modern-day prophets and Apostles, as well as the scriptures, will help us find needed answers and learn truth—truth that will make all the difference in our struggles.

During a particularly difficult time in college, I clung to the words of Elder Richard G. Scott from his October 1995 general conference talk. Sitting in my apartment, I watched his television address. He lovingly gazed into the camera as he spoke, and I knew he was speaking directly to me. His words about life's trials brought peace to my heart and eased my worried mind. As an Apostle of Christ, he taught the world true doctrine:

"Just when all seems to be going right, challenges often come in multiple doses applied simultaneously. When those trials are not consequences of your disobedience, they are evidence that the Lord feels you are prepared to grow more (see Prov. 3:11–12). He therefore gives you experiences that stimulate growth, understanding, and compassion which polish you for your everlasting benefit. To get you from where you are to where He wants you to be requires a lot of stretching, and that generally entails discomfort and pain" ("Trust in the Lord," *Ensign*, November 1995, 16).

With those words, I knew that Father was aware of my suffering. I was definitely experiencing things that would "stimulate growth." The pain and discomfort that I was feeling was absolutely stretching me. In fact, I'm sure I have spiritual stretch marks to prove it. "Multiple doses" of trials seemed to describe my life at that time. It seemed that I was bombarded with physical and emotional challenges, and I longed for a reprieve.

The words of Christ's Apostle reinforced to me that Heavenly Father was trying to help me move from my current position to where I needed to be. Because the difficulty I was experiencing was not caused from sin, I could trust that it was, as Elder Scott said, "evidence that the Lord [felt that I was] prepared to grow more."

I have to admit that I didn't jump up and down in celebration that I was hurting while being refined. I didn't cheer, "Wahoo! I get to grow more!" But I felt better knowing that the trial had an eternal reason and benefit, even if I did not understand it. I really did want to be polished, so I guess I did need the trial after all. Elder Scott's words, which I read over and over again, became a holy place and strengthened my connection to my Savior.

When I study the Book of Mormon, I often find doctrine that helps me better understand my trials. The pages of this record are filled with the accounts of men and women who experienced great hardships, and I love to learn from their actions. When adversity comes, some turn almost automatically to the Lord for strength. Others turn away. When the Nephites or Lamanites turn to sin rather than to God, I feel like yelling, "Don't be stupid! Just turn to God and things will work out!" But then I realize that they are dead and won't hear me anyway.

One account in the Book of Mormon that teaches me truths about trials is that of the brother of Jared. I have learned a great deal by discovering what he and his people did when swallowed by hardship. I find it significant that their difficulties were actually what furthered their progress to the promised land. In Ether 6, we read of how they followed the direction of the Lord:

"They got aboard of their vessels or barges, and set forth into the sea, commending themselves unto the Lord their God. And it came to pass that the Lord God caused that there should be a furious wind blow upon the face of the waters, towards the promised land; and thus they were tossed upon the waves of the sea before the wind" (Ether 6:4–5).

First, incredibly, they "commend[ed] themselves unto the Lord." In essence, you or I might have said, "Here I am, Lord. I now put myself, my life, my future, my everything in your hands. I don't know what will happen, but I trust you completely." I can't imagine getting into those barges that were "tight like unto a dish" (Ether 6:7). It sounds a lot like the MRI tubes I have spent so much time in. Talk about claustrophobia! But that's exactly what these followers of Christ did. They commended themselves to the Lord. What a lesson for me.

Next, the "furious wind" began to blow. The Lord was in control of the wind, and yet He "caused" it to blow. Would you or I have complained and said, "You have got to be kidding me! I trusted you enough to get into this dish and now I'm being tossed on the waves by a wind you sent on purpose?" But look at the direction of the wind. It blew "towards the promised land." That is phenomenal! The Lord directed the barges and propelled them with the fierce winds. He actually caused their progress. That was the purpose of the wind.

Sometimes I feel overwhelmed by adversity and trials, but I can think of the Jaredites, faithfully allowing the Lord to get them to their destination. The winds never stopped. Never. I sometimes wish that the pain or sorrow I feel would just stop. However, if my trials all ceased when I asked for them to, it would stunt my spiritual growth. It would be like the Jaredites getting sick of the winds and asking the Lord to make them cease. They would be stuck somewhere in the ocean with no way of progressing toward their promised land.

Even though it must have been tremendously difficult, they trusted in, prayed to, and praised the One who was causing the trial. What could have been nearly a year-long complaining session, or a time of bitterness and blaming God, really was a time of holiness and progression.

What a tremendous blueprint for me to follow when I am swallowed up in trial. I understand that trials and difficulties can actually propel me to my promised land.

If my hardships are not a result of sin, they really are designed for my eternal good. It is a loving Father who allows difficulties to come, and it is a loving Father who helps us during the tempest. The ferocious winds do and will blow. It is not just a trite phrase. It is true. The winds that blow, and the waves that crash down upon us, sometimes seem unbearable. Sometimes, the word *overwhelming* is an understatement. Hard times, challenging times, miserable times come to us and, if you are like me, you wonder if and how you can make it through. We fought for these times as part of Father's plan, and now, ironically, we have to fight through them.

When the winds blow, it can be hard to detect the progress they create. It can just feel like we are being swallowed up by the gale forces. In the fall of 1994, I went through such an experience. I certainly felt the storm, but I didn't feel I was learning, growing, or moving toward the Father. I was just suffering. Not until after the trial did I see my progress.

As a single student at Brigham Young University, I began having severe head pain, dizziness, and fainting. I was taken to the emergency room and had several CT scans. Nothing unusual showed on the scans and the doctors said to return if the problem didn't go away in a few days. Well, the problem became worse. I was in so much pain that I couldn't function. Another ER trip proved fruitless in diagnosing and treating the problem correctly. One extremely pain-filled day, I went desperately to a doctor in the urgent-care clinic on campus. That doctor told me that I had made up the pain to get myself out of taking finals. He prescribed a bottle of Valium and sent me on my way to get over it.

I was so upset! I couldn't take the pain and frustration anymore. No one could help me. I called home, crying to my parents. They flew me back home to California and had me seen by our family physician. Another CT scan and a whole lot more pain occurred before I finally was diagnosed correctly.

After the scan, my doctor, also a personal friend, said, "Kris, you aren't going to want to hear this, but you are a diagnosed airhead." He wasn't being rude, just finding a little humor in a very serious matter. The films of my head showed that air had gotten inside my brain, which had been the cause of the debilitating pain. I really was an "airhead." Cerebral spinal fluid was leaking out my nose, coming from a large tear in my brain covering, and there was a large crack in a bone inside my skull.

I was referred to the head of neurosurgery at Stanford University Medical Center, the hospital where I had been treated with radiation as an infant. Here, I underwent an excruciating brain surgery to fix the problem. This craniotomy entailed opening up my forehead, grafting donor tissue into my brain covering, and wiring closed the cracked bone. It was a horrendous experience. The following months were so painful. My progress in recovery seemed nonexistent. I wondered why, when I prayed so fervently, I was not improving. My suffering was constant and I longed for restored health and freedom from pain. I became extremely discouraged.

During my long recovery, it seemed that Heavenly Father was far away. I desired the pain to be removed or at least eased; however, it took many long months of suffering before I was better. I wondered what I was to learn from this experience.

Finally, the Spirit taught me that I was learning to suffer like Christ. Wow! That hit me hard. Of course, my suffering could not compare to His, but, in my realm of pain, I learned to submit to the will of the Father, as Christ did. That was the purpose I held on to. That bit of understanding and insight brought me closer to Christ, and, at the end of a horrible experience, my spiritual tutorial built a holy place. Wasn't it, then, worth the pain? Although my body screams "No!" my spirit knows absolutely that the answer is "Yes!" The painful winds were bringing me closer to my promised land—my Heavenly Father.

There are some trials that won't go away in this life. When it is the Father's will, struggles and hardship are right. Fasting, prayer, and faith will not remove those difficulties that God sees fit for our growth. When we find out Father's will concerning us, our faith and prayers will be focused on doing His will instead of changing it.

We may not feel like we have enough faith to have a trial removed. But it may take even more faith to live with the trial than to have it lifted from us. There are burdens Father will remove upon our asking, according to His will, but we should not expect Him to alter what is best for us every time we ask. If He did so, we would not be able to return to or become like Him.

Our hard times have an eternal purpose and can anchor us to Christ. As you and I commend ourselves unto the Lord and allow the winds of tribulation to move us closer to Him, we will be in the strongest position to receive His help and power to weather the storms.

Chapter Five

TRUST ON

There is so much more to me than eye problems, but since I wear my troubles on the outside where they are seen, that is what I am judged by. This was painfully true during my dating years. Although I was the coolest girl around—well, at least I thought so—I was not considered someone to date. I had many, many guy friends but was no one's love. I think I should have an honorary counseling degree for the amount of time I spent guiding boys through relationships; however, those relationships never involved me. Why couldn't guys see the whole me?

I didn't sit around moping about my lack of social prospects—all right, sometimes I did—but I tried to remain happy and trust in the promises I had been given in my patriarchal blessing. I trusted Christ to fill my aching heart with His love and peace until the time when God's promises were fulfilled.

In college I dated quite a bit but had several heart-breaking situations. I even had one guy who explained that he had taken me out because he felt sorry for me. I was on his list of girls to take out as "good deeds." This, obviously, did not go over well with my heart. It was difficult for me to trust other men when they invited me out on dates. I would wonder, "Does he really like me, or just feel sorry for me?"

Other guys loved me—some even admitted it—but they always got hung up on the eye issue. I was told often that I "had it all, except . . ." I wasn't packaged quite right. My facial abnormalities and limited vision always prevented relationships from going anywhere.

Still, I trusted and waited, trying not to allow my heart to become bitter. I waited on the Lord and moved forward in my schooling and with my life. I served a mission in Kentucky. I worked on my degree. And I ached inside for someone to share my life and my love. Trust in Christ helped me not to give up.

And then, there was James. When he expressed a desire to have a more serious relationship, I doubted he would stick around; after all, no one else had. During one of our "talks," I gave him the long list of my physical problems and waited for his reaction and quick departure. "Yeah, and?" was his response. This guy wasn't scared off. In fact, he was serious. I couldn't believe it! James wasn't hindered in the least by the problems with my eyes, nor by the possibility of more physical difficulties in the future.

I fasted, prayed, and trusted that I would be led in my decisions concerning James and our relationship. When he proposed marriage, I pled for guidance in the matter. I was told in a priesthood blessing that James had been prepared for me and would make me happy—but that if I didn't want to marry him, another man would be provided for me.

Heavenly Father was so good to me. For so many years, my heart had been cradled in His healing hands, and now His promised blessings were being fulfilled. I didn't "have" to marry James, but I wanted to.

The day we were married for time and eternity in the Salt Lake Temple was the best day of my life. The ceremony was so beautiful inside that holy place. Hundreds of people joined us at the reception to celebrate our union, and I have never had so much fun.

Waiting on the Lord and trusting Him for so many years had brought me to this wonderful point. Now, together, James and I would continue to trust as we made our way forward through life.

Several years later, we found that we were pregnant. Unfortunately, but not surprisingly, my body did not handle pregnancy well. It began breaking its own tissues down in order to feed the baby. I was miserable, bedridden, nauseated, constantly throwing up, and in danger of losing my life. My doctor and home health nurses struggled in an effort to stabilize my condition, but nothing worked. Finally, an I.V. was inserted into a vein in my chest, and all of my nutrition and medications were injected through it.

Every agonizing second passed so slowly; I didn't think I could make it nine whole months like this. Again, I placed my trust and faith in Jesus Christ. I prayed that Heavenly Father would grant me the ability to endure the situation in order to bring one of His spirits to the earth.

There came a critical point when my doctor said, "If your body is not stabilized by tomorrow, we'll have to take the baby." I was crushed at this declaration and prayed even more fervently. My family fasted and prayed for my improvement, and, mercifully, it wasn't necessary to abort the baby. How grateful I was for this blessing! It was another holy place.

I fought through the entire pregnancy in bed, taking anti-nausea medication every four hours. Finally, our little Christopher was born. There were some complications at his birth, and he had to remain in the Newborn Intensive Care Unit (N.I.C.U.) for several weeks. This tore my heart apart. But together James and I trusted in the Lord and in the Father's will. Through the power of the priesthood, our new little boy lived and was able to come home with us.

Because the pregnancy had been so incredibly difficult, and both my life and Christopher's life had been at risk, we doubted we would have another baby. We determined that it would take clear instructions from Heavenly Father in order for us to go through that experience again.

Well, guess what? Four years later we received our clear instructions. Once again, I became pregnant and deathly ill. Again I struggled through the long months until, six weeks early, Benjamin decided to join the family. He was just over five pounds, but seemed healthy, and James and I were excited this time to be able to take our baby home.

But, in the middle of the night, a nurse entered my

hospital room and explained that Benjamin would have to be taken by ambulance to the children's hospital in Salt Lake City for surgery. It was explained that in utero, Benji's intestine, unknown to anyone, had herniated up into the umbilical cord. When the doctor had cut Benji's cord, he had severed his intestine as well.

We pled with the Father to spare our little baby boy and to help him through the operation. Benjamin did come through the surgery, but because of complications he was admitted to the N.I.C.U. For several days, I was in one hospital and our baby was in another, many miles away. I couldn't hold or help my little boy. My empty arms and troubled heart longed to be with my suffering baby. Again, all I could do was trust in my Savior. I knew that whatever happened, Christ would be with me.

Fortunately, Benji pulled out of danger and was released from the N.I.C.U. after three weeks. But during most of the time in those three weeks, which seemed like three months filled with long hours of worry, I was able to be right at my baby's side. Friends and family members drove me the hour-long trip each day while others cared for Christopher, then four years old. It was a difficult ordeal, both physically, recovering from another C-section, and emotionally, constantly worrying about my sick little baby connected to a labyrinth of tubes and machines. Yet my Savior was constantly there to lift and comfort me and my sweet family.

Trust in Christ was also necessary to help us face other issues. Earlier in my life, I had been warned that I should not have children. Retinoblastoma is a genetically inherited disease, and my doctor counseled me to abort my baby if I ever became pregnant. This suggestion disgusted and upset me, and I declared that I would never do that to my child. I wasn't going to take my baby's life because he or she had eye cancer. What if my mother had done that? My life, though difficult, was worth living. If Heavenly Father wanted me to give birth, then I would do it.

After Christopher was born, he had to be examined for retinoblastoma. Every two months, he was anesthetized, and his eyes were checked for any sign of tumors. This was incredibly difficult for us as his parents. For years, every couple of months, James and I took our little boy to the hospital and prayed there would be no cancer. I trusted in my Savior and tried to exercise my faith. I felt responsible for the predicament and hoped this horrible disease would not be passed on to him. For more than four years,

Christopher was examined, and, fortunately, he stayed free of cancer.

In the year before I became pregnant with Benjamin, I went through some genetic testing, and the retino-blastoma gene was isolated on my DNA. After Benji's birth, a sample of blood was drawn from him and from Christopher for testing. The lab found that Benjamin did not carry the gene, but Christopher did. So, while we were relieved about our new baby, we worried about Christopher, who still had to go through exams.

Several months later, we were informed that the labs had mistakenly switched the blood samples. I was floored and furious. Things like this happened only on TV. It was Benji, not Christopher, who carried the retinoblastoma gene. Christopher had needlessly gone through another general anesthetic, and my infant, who really was at risk, had not been checked. Precious time had been lost due to this needless mistake. Early detection is vital in treating the disease successfully, and I prayed that my baby's life would not be endangered on account of the lab's negligence.

During the time Benjamin was in the operating room for his first exam, I prayed with all my heart and tried to trust in Christ. When the surgeon came to give us the results, he was amazed and relieved. He had really thought he would find cancer in my baby's eyes, but he had not. We had received another miracle! Every few months from then until he was five, we took Benji for examinations under anesthesia. Each time, we prayed and trusted, and each time, we received good news. Although he carried the gene, Benjamin did not have the disease. Now that he is over five years old, he can be checked less frequently, and in the ophthalmologist's office. I don't know what the future will hold, but I trust the Savior to carry us through.

He will do the same for you. Please know that you need not carry your burdens alone. The Savior has already suffered what you are suffering. He has felt the deepest pain imaginable and does know how to help. Trust Him. Don't let Satan convince you to give in to sorrow and despair, but trust in the arm of the Lord. He will support you in your trials, and in your troubles, and in your afflictions (see Alma 36:3). Trust Christ, and He will become your holy place.

Chapter Six

THE TRIAL OF MY LIFE

I remember the morning, a few weeks before Christmas 2003, when I first realized my vision was in serious trouble. My husband and I had just opened a flower shop in Lehi, Utah, and were doing everything we knew to advertise our infant business. I had arranged for James, who is an amazingly talented florist, to appear on the morning news broadcast of a local television station. At 4:30 A.M. we drove to Salt Lake for him to demonstrate how to use flowers in Christmas decorating. As we set up the flowers and other supplies, I remember wondering why they didn't turn on some lights in the studio. I could barely see anything, and I had to hold onto James as we walked. There was about the same amount of light as is typically emitted from a night-light, and I didn't know how they all could function in the dimness. The camera guy thought I was crazy when I asked him if they would turn on more lights when it was time to film James. He explained that he'd have one more bright light on, but that there was plenty of light already in the studio. Well, I thought he was the one who was crazy until James and I were back in the car. As we talked, I learned that all the bright lights had been on the whole time.

I could not believe it. There was something definitely wrong. It was then that I began the fight to reclaim my vision. I feared the future and what it might hold for me, but I had no idea that the future I so dreaded would soon become my permanent present.

Several visits to eye specialists proved fruitless. No one could find a reason for my vision loss. One specialist, because he could find no evidence, made me feel that my change in vision was imagined. However, I continued seeking reasons for my fading world.

A few days before Christmas, I sat in my living room with my husband and his parents. Everyone was talking and sharing gifts, except for me. I had tuned out from the noise and chatter. During this moment of internal quiet, I felt a voice inside tell me I needed to get a CT scan. That spiritual communication became a true holy place. I then knew what direction to go to find the solution to my vision mystery.

However, my doctor would not order the scan. A few days later, tremendous head pain greeted me when I woke up, and I knew I had to get that CT scan immediately, so my husband and I rushed to the emergency room. Still, the doctors and radiologists found nothing that would explain my vision loss or severe head pain. Fortunately, I was referred to the ophthalmologist on call, who took a long time to ask me questions and examine the films from the scan.

Then he said, "There is something in your eye socket that shouldn't be there."

What was it that was in my eye socket? A bean? A Lego? Unfortunately, I knew exactly what it was. It was cancer. This doctor had found the culprit, and the thing I had feared for years was right before my eyes; well, actually, it was growing behind my eyes and up into my sinuses. I would have to undergo surgery.

My insurance company insisted I go to a new doctor, who, after more tests, decided to operate immediately. It was ten o'clock at night by the time I was wheeled down the long hall to the operating room. James was permitted to walk alongside the gurney, and this brought me comfort. When we reached the place where he was to leave me, I looked at his shadowy outline, felt his kiss on my cheek, and heard his loving, sentimental final words: "Be good!" Well, that wasn't quite what I was looking for—I'll have to write him a script for future departure scenes—but I knew he loved me, even if he didn't say it.

I was wheeled the rest of the way down the hall and left alone right outside the operating room. I lay there, listening to the sounds of the hospital, and prayed fervently. I pleaded with my Father in Heaven that the surgeon would be assisted and that my vision would be saved. I wanted so desperately to see James and my boys again. That place in the hospital hallway was illuminated by dim lights, or at least it seemed so to me. I had no idea that was the last time I would see anything at all, dim or otherwise.

A tumor, about the size of a double peanut in a shell, was removed. It was determined to have been caused by the radiation treatments from my infancy, and my surgeon felt very confident that all the cancer had come out encapsulated. I was so grateful to have this cancer business finished—or so I thought.

Lying there in the hospital bed, I grew increasingly alarmed. Before the procedure, I had been able to see a little bit; now, afterward, I saw absolutely nothing. What had gone wrong?

When I consulted with my surgeon, he explained that the blindness was temporary. Postoperative swelling was pushing on my optic nerve, resulting in my vision loss. He said that as soon as the swelling subsided, I would see again. Well, that sounded good to me. I could be patient and wait for the light to return. I placed my hope and confidence in the knowledge and skill of this kind man.

I was released from the hospital a week later, and I imagined that things would improve as I recovered. Did I mention the story about the rabbit fur coat? Again, my expectations came nowhere near reality.

After a follow-up CT scan to ensure all the cancer was gone, I was informed that there was more tumor behind my right eye. I was absolutely devastated. I recall breaking down right there in the hospital with my sister. There was no way this was really happening!

Additionally, the scan showed air bubbles, indicating a cerebral spinal fluid leak. The covering of my brain, damaged and weakened by my childhood radiation, had been affected by the recent surgery near that area. Once again, I was an airhead.

Over the phone, my surgeon and I discussed the test results. He had just been in that very area and removed the entire tumor; therefore, he disagreed with the radiologist's findings. He reassured me that what they were seeing behind my eye was not tumor but swelling. I was relieved with the news; however, there was that airhead issue.

Off I went, in immense pain, to the E.N.T. neurosurgeon for an evaluation and subsequent surgery. This surgeon performed an intricate brain operation through my nose, grafting cartilage into my brain covering to plug the spinal fluid leak.

Part of the recovery from this operation consisted of lying with my head at a particular angle with a drain in my spine. This was necessary to pull the spinal fluid away from the graft site so it could seal properly. Words cannot describe the kind of pain I experienced. I was weak from the previous month's surgery, and here I was trying to cope with incredible head pain. Mind you, I was still blind.

Before I was released from this week-and-a-half hospital stay, an M.R.I. was ordered. I knew I was not up to this test with the intense head pain I was experiencing and asked to be allowed to postpone it for a few days. But, with a stern tone, my E.N.T. neurosurgeon insisted. It was absolutely urgent that I have the M.R.I. that very day—my life depended on it.

Crying because of the pain from my spinal headache, I was loaded into the M.R.I. tube and instructed not to move. Then the machine-gun-like sounds began all around me. The noise from the machine hurt me so badly, I fought hard not to panic. I remember begging Heavenly Father to help me through the test and to enable me to remain calm. He gave me the peace I needed to endure, minute by minute. I made it through that experience and was released to go home.

My case, including the M.R.I. results and films, was then discussed at a meeting of local cancer specialists and radiologists. At this "cancer board," difficult cases were presented and a treatment plan was proposed by these experts. From my scans, it was determined that I indeed had another tumor behind my eye. There was no postoperative swelling. If I was to have a chance at survival, the tumor had to be removed immediately.

When my eye surgeon explained this to me, I again

crumbled emotionally. He informed me that the large mass was located on my optic nerve, which travels through thin bone directly to the brain. I was told that my eye would have to be removed and the optic nerve as well. If it was left for too long, the cancer would travel the path of the nerve right to my brain. It might have already done so.

Oh, how I prayed. I cried to Heavenly Father to help me through this horrible experience. I knew that He had all power and could absolutely heal me. I had complete faith in Him and begged for this miracle. Of course, I did pray for His will to be done, but I longed for my healing to be His will.

In addition to praying like crazy, I sought additional opinions from my previous eye doctors. In one office, my mother and I sat, nervous and anxious, awaiting the doctor's evaluation of my scans. To my utter devastation, he too proposed the immediate removal of the tumor and my eye. I begged for another solution, but there was none. Either I could leave my eye in place and die, or have the eye and tumor removed and possibly survive. I was in total shock.

Back in the car, I phoned my husband at work with the horrible news. All I could do was weep. After my phone call, my mother asked where I wanted to go. I wanted—no, *needed*—to go to Temple Square. We drove the few blocks in sorrow for my inevitable future. Together we made our way to the North Visitors' Center to the Christus statue. There, symbolically standing at the feet of the Savior, I wept. I longed to be able to open my eyes and see the outstretched arms of Jesus. I wished I could kneel before Him and be healed like those He had touched in the scriptures. I stood there, emotionally traumatized, physically spent, and spiritually searching. I needed help.

For over an hour, we sat on a bench at the back of the rotunda area. I wondered how I would ever do this. If I survived, how could I live my life blind? This was not the way things were supposed to go! My strength was gone, and I questioned how much more I could take.

I pled for peace, for strength, and for the love of Christ to enfold me. Over and over, in many languages, I listened to the recording of the words of Christ from the scriptures being played in that sacred place. My heart caught hold of six little words and I wondered at their truth. The voice representing Christ spoke to my heart, saying, "Let not your heart be troubled." How could this be? I had just received the news that if I survived the cancer, I would be completely blind. My heart was just plain devastated. How could I not "let" it be troubled? What was I to do?

As I pondered and prayed for strength, peace entered my heart. I knew the answer. I needed, again, to turn it all over to Christ. Although I could not see the Christus statue, Jesus Christ could see me. He knew me and would continue to assist me through the pain and darkness. He could heal my heart and it wouldn't have to remain troubled. Once again, Christ was my answer.

That day, I found a holy place at the foot of the Christus statue.

Leaving that holy place, I was led to another. Arm in arm, my mother and I walked eastward to the Salt Lake Temple. Here, I placed my hands on the stone wall and tried to gain courage. That building represented so much to me. The rock of the temple felt sturdy, even mighty. I leaned my back against it and thought of the covenants I had made inside that very edifice.

In this sacred place, I had knelt at a holy altar and been sealed to my sweet James. I had seen the tears in his eyes as the ceremony was performed and had seen his goodness. I would never see him again in this life. It hurt terribly! I knew, however, that no matter if I lived or died, was blind or sighted, we would be together after this life if we were faithful. I knew that the two little boys I fought so hard to live for would be ours forever as well. I would never again see the faces of my wonderful sons in mortality, but I clung to the knowledge that I would see them in the life to come. That knowledge did not remove the sorrow, but it gave me hope to take the next step in this treacherous journey.

I touched the smoothness of the temple granite and remembered the pioneers. I thought of the weary hands that had labored tirelessly to construct this temple and how much the people were asked to sacrifice. I too was being asked to sacrifice. I would have to give up my sight and perhaps my life, but my offering was more than this. The sacrifice hardest to give was my will. There, at this sacred temple, I figuratively placed my will on God's altar. All my desires for vision, my expectations and dreams for my future, even my life, I gave to Him. If I had to lose my vision to live and raise my children with my husband, I was willing to do it. It was evidently not Heavenly Father's will for my sight to be spared. It might not even be His will that I remain on the earth, but at last I was able to say, "Thy will be done," and mean it.

On the day of the dreaded surgery, James and I sat together in the hospital pre-op room. I tried so hard to be brave. To help me go forward with this procedure, I recalled the words of a priesthood blessing given to me that morning. I was nervous but calm. That is, I was calm until the nurse instructed me to write the word "yes" above my right eye with a marker to indicate which eye was to be removed. I completely fell apart. There was no way I could do what she asked. I couldn't even take the pen from her hand. All I could do was weep frantically. I didn't want to give up my eye. How could I do this? Marking my eye was like marking the end of all I knew. My life would never be the same. Sweetly, James took the pen and marked my skin above the brow. He did what I could not do. I was so grateful for him.

As I was wheeled into surgery to have my right eye removed, I received the startling truth. I asked my surgeon where he would make the incision, and he used his finger to draw a circle around my eye.

"What about my eyelid?" I panicked.

My new reality was that I would have no eyelids, nor would I have any tissue, muscles, or nerves in my eye socket. Anything and everything that might have been exposed to the cancer cells had to be removed. This would make it impossible for me to wear an artificial eye.

"What will I do?" I asked my surgeon in complete alarm.

He told me that I could either wear a black patch— you know, the kind a pirate would wear—or get a pair of glasses with an eyeball attached. When I put on the glasses, the fake eyeball would just pop into my socket.

Well, we were going from bad to worse. I was frantic at this point. I started sobbing uncontrollably and had to be sedated as I entered the operating room.

The surgery was performed and I again awoke to darkness; however, this time, I knew the darkness was permanent. Once again, I began the process of both physical and emotional recovery.

It is difficult, emotionally, to articulate what I felt after this procedure. I had never known such sorrow and complete devastation. My life and everything I knew had been turned upside down. Without sight, my independence was gone. I had not yet gained the skills needed to function in a world of darkness, and I needed someone to guide my every step. I felt alone on the inside, but on the outside I couldn't function by myself. I felt trapped in the dark and very claustrophobic.

I found myself drowning in a deeper level of emotions than ever before. Now that my right eye had been removed, I felt un-whole. It was like a part of my very core had been yanked out as well. My head knew I was still complete, but my heart definitely disagreed. I felt that I had a huge cavern in my head and in my soul. I was grossed out by what my face had become and felt positive everyone else was too. Of course, my eye socket was covered with a patch, but I still felt everyone was disgusted. I could not comprehend how my husband could still love me, or why he would even want to touch me. My very person, it seemed, was damaged beyond repair. How was I to live like this?

Unfortunately, that was not the end of the difficulty. The tissue biopsy came back with good news and bad news. Once again, over the phone, my surgeon explained the results. The cancer had not yet traveled to my brain via my optic nerve; however, tissue from my sinus area showed traces of the disease. I was still not out of the woods. Another more invasive and difficult operation was required to keep the cancer from invading my brain from the sinus region.

I was absolutely distraught. I couldn't do it! There was no way I could endure another surgery and more pain. I felt like one of those smiling clown punching bags I had played with as a child—the ones you punch over and over again, and each time they pop back up, still smiling. The trouble was that each time I was knocked down I couldn't heal enough to get back up completely.

There was definitely no smile left on this clown, yet the punches kept coming.

This time, four surgeons, led by Heavenly Father, were required to perform the needed miracle. My life was at stake, and I braced myself for the seven-hour surgery. The O.R. staff was, by now, very familiar with me, as were the nurses in pre-op. I felt I should get a surgery discount with all the frequent-scalpel miles I had accrued.

I was wheeled, again, into the operating room. I won't go into all the gory details, but this major craniotomy was my last chance to prevent the cancer from spreading to my brain, and the surgeons did all they could to preserve my life.

The scriptural phrase "weeping, and wailing, and

gnashing of teeth" (Alma 40:13) sums up my time in the hospital following the operation. For several weeks, day after day, I wrestled with physical and emotional devastation. I remember hearing a patient in another room complain about the moaning noises he heard across the hall. Then I realized he was talking about me. Involuntarily, I was moaning out loud. I hurt so deeply, inside and out. I was mourning and crying from my very soul. It sounds strange, but that was all I could do. Every bit of me was in agony.

The results of the tissue and bone biopsies, this time, came back clear of cancer. At last, some good news!

When I was stable enough, I was released to go home, and, again, I began the recovery process. But the poor clown punching bag, still on the floor, received another sock in the face: I noticed symptoms of a spinal fluid leak, and feared what that meant. It was true; I had another leak.

Back I went for yet another brain surgery. Once more, I lay miserably in the hospital with my head at a particular angle and a drain in my spine. I truly wondered if the pain and suffering would ever end. There was no strength left within me.

This marathon of tests, doctor evaluations, surgeries, hospitalizations, and pseudo-recoveries lasted nearly six months. The physical and emotional pain was indescribably awful. Miraculously, my life was preserved. It was Heavenly Father's will for me to survive; and now I would rely on Him to show me how to live.

Chapter Seven

MY HOLY PLACE OF HEALING

E ach time I read the Book of Mormon account of Christ visiting the Nephites, I long to have been among the multitude. The Savior showed so much compassion as He extended an invitation of healing: "Have ye any that are sick among you? Bring them hither. Have ye any that are lame, or blind, or halt, or maimed, or leprous, or that are withered, or that are deaf, or that are afflicted in any manner? Bring them hither and I will heal them" (3 Nephi 17:7).

If I had been present, I would have jumped up and down with excitement and gratitude, insisting to be brought to His side. At His touch, my eyes would have been opened, and I would have looked into His eyes with perfect vision. But this is my time to be alive, and my complete healing must wait for the resurrection.

One by one, the multitude approached Christ and were healed. Similarly, one by one, we can approach our Father in Heaven through prayer for needed healing. Times of sincere prayer can be sweet times of healing. Many times, as I have poured out my sorrows, I have felt the Spirit wrap itself around my broken and troubled heart. Awareness and understanding have filled my mind, and I have known I would be all right. These experiences have provided needed emotional healing.

I have also petitioned Heavenly Father to grant me healing for my physical body. Because I want to become like Him, I know I have to be stretched and changed, and it is through trials that this can occur. Therefore, even though I want to, I cannot always ask for every problem or pain to be removed or completely healed and still expect to be as polished and perfected as He is.

I am reminded of an experience I had as a teenager at a stake girls camp. I was one of twenty or more girls on a hike, estimated to be four to five miles long, in the Sierra Nevada Mountains. Five miles had come and gone, and each time we ascended a difficult climb, our leader would say, "It's all downhill from here, girls." After a while we grew suspicious. The "uphills" kept coming, yet we never found our camp. We wondered if he really knew where we were. However, we were always assured that our challenging climb would soon be at an end. After a while his promise, "It's all downhill from here," became a joke. Finally he admitted to being lost.

So there we were, a large group of young women being led through rough terrain, and our leaders didn't have a clue how to get us out of our predicament. The short hike ended up being more than twenty miles long. It was extremely difficult to carry heavy packs up and down mountain trails and not know when the ordeal would be over.

Because of my poor vision, a friend hiked in front of me to warn me of trouble spots. Nevertheless, I ended up twisting both ankles and had to continue the hike in pain.

Gratefully, in answer to our many prayers, help arrived. A helicopter from the power company landed in a field near us, with a warning. Several of the dams in the area were being opened and water levels would rise drastically. Our group would have to get to higher ground.

Our leader got directions from the power workers, so

now we would be able to make our way to our destination. However, before the power workers left, my leader came to me and explained that I would be returning via helicopter along with another girl in our group with poor health. The rest of the hikers would meet us back at the power station.

I was livid! I had not come this far, only to be denied the chance to finish. But my leader logically explained that the group would be able to travel faster through the treacherous climb ahead if they did not have to care for us.

Angrily I boarded the chopper and watched all my friends below turn into ant-sized dots as the helicopter gained altitude. The view was magnificent as we flew effortlessly over lakes, rivers, green forests, and open meadows, but the beauty was lost on me. I was too furious that I had been taken away from finishing my difficult hike with my friends. It was only years later that I realized that I had been the lucky one. I had been spared further pain and struggle. I had literally been lifted out of my trial.

I think about this experience sometimes when I want so desperately to be lifted out of my difficulties. It seems so right that Heavenly Father should heal my hurts, remove my obstacles, and lift my burdens. But if He did so with every petition, I would not "come off conqueror" (D&C

10:5). There is great purpose in my experiencing and overcoming my trials.

I also know that Father has certain blessings that He wants to give me, but that are conditioned upon my asking for them. In prayer I can go to Him, tell Him my desires, and say, "Please let me know Thy will concerning me in this situation. Are my desires for healing in accordance with Thine?" If I continue in this attitude, the answers will come. They have come.

Father has answered me as I have prayed. Sometimes, the answer was that it was not His will to heal me. On occasion, He has taken a portion of the problem away. And other times, God has lightened my burden or made me strong enough to bear it. A few times, Heavenly Father has even seen fit to remove the problem completely.

Throughout the long, traumatic months of cancer surgeries and blindness, I prayed constantly for healing—healing for both my emotional and physical misery. Family members, neighbors, friends, my entire ward, and even people I had never met, all fasted and prayed for me to receive the gift of healing. I desired a miracle so desperately, yet I lost my remaining vision and suffered terribly in body and mind. It was the most difficult time of my life. Where was the healing from Him who was my Healer?

Some might say that this needed healing blessing was denied me, but I know differently. Heavenly healing did come; however, it arrived in ways I never imagined. True, I didn't receive a miraculous cure, but I was healed. The most important healing came from each holy place along my difficult, painful path. When I felt I was falling apart, I received healing comfort and power to move forward. The broken pieces of my heart were rearranged and, with time, put back together. There were sacred times when I felt heaven near. The love of my Savior and Heavenly Father provided immense healing to my desperate soul. Prayer was my salve and priesthood blessings were my balm of reassurance and direction.

After my last brain surgery, I wondered many times a day, "How am I going to make it through this? I can't do it!" I had gone through so much and didn't have the capacity on my own to move forward. First, I begged Father to help me have the strength to just sit up in my bed. Then I asked for strength to stand, and then to walk a few steps. This process of seeking healing and strength continued for months.

With tremendous help and patience from my mother, my husband, and healing from above, I did make improvement. Slowly, the physical pain diminished to a manageable constant hurt. It took over a year before I felt somewhat functional.

Emotionally, I had a long way to go to be well. I went through a real grieving process for many months. I grieved for my lost eye, for my lost vision, for my lost health, and for my lost dreams and expectations. I had to work through disappointment, anger, and despair. I wondered when I would be myself again. Where was the happy, hopeful high school cheerleader who was voted "Most Optimistic"? The light inside, as well as outside, seemed to have been extinguished.

But gradually, healing also came for my emotions. Each tiny step of progress built upon the last.

Healing even came through the scalpel. Each surgery I endured brought me closer to the extinction of the invading cancer. It wasn't until recently that I was even able to perceive this as healing. I had prayed for the surgeons to be led in saving my life, and they were. Surgery was definitely not the type of healing I hoped for, but it accomplished the will of the Lord. Talented surgeons enabled me to remain a mother to my boys and a wife to my husband.

Also, a tremendous amount of healing came through the love and service of members of my ward. So many acts of kindness were performed on my behalf and that of my family. My sweet visiting teachers cleaned my house every Tuesday for months. My boys were cared for by my ward friends, as they shared shifts with my sisters and parents. I received many phone calls, gifts, treats, visits, and even a surprise birthday party. Additionally, many people came to visit me in the hospital, located nearly an hour away. Most important, I felt so blessed that I was kept in the thoughts and prayers of so many people. I know that healing came through those prayers of faith.

Meals were brought in for so long that I think my husband was dreading the day I'd be able to cook again. He became a connoisseur of casseroles and found his favorite chefs in the ward. James has never liked my cooking nearly as much since he was spoiled by the kindness of others.

Several months following my last brain surgery, I was given a gift by one of my closest friends and her sweet husband, which made all the difference in my recovery and healing. As soon as my body had enough strength, they sent us to southern California for some rest and recuperation.

While James and I sat on the beach, I felt the pent-up tension and strain begin to wash away. The previous months' trauma seemed to be carried away with the waves as they left the shore.

It was difficult not to be able to see the ocean, which I love, but the sound of the crashing waves brought me comfort and erased the troubles that filled my mind. As the waves crashed, I was reminded of the power of God. In all His greatness and power, He loved me. I had been preserved to live, and sitting there with the sand beneath my feet, I felt a little hope for my future. The sorrow started to drain away, and my courage was magnified. I cried silently for all I had suffered, for all I still had to endure, and in gratitude for the love and strength of my Savior. That spot on the beach is a holy place of healing. I am so grateful for kind friends who graciously gave me the opportunity to really begin my emotional healing process.

My heart was also healed, a little at a time, by the sweet concern of my husband and children. Their love gave me courage to press forward. My older son's excitement for life and compassion for my pain warmed my troubled heart. Healing warmth entered my soul when my baby smiled at me. Although I could no longer see it, I could sense his smile and hear it in his laughter. I told myself many times a day that it was worth the struggle to stay alive so that I could raise these little boys and be a wife to James.

The night I found out I had cancer, I needed my siblings around me. I called my brothers and sisters who lived locally, and they came over immediately. Each of my five siblings has always been a solid source of strength to me, and they are among my best friends. Their friendship and selflessness, as always, buoyed me up and brought me encouragement. Even though they told me when I was little that I was found under a rock, I am eternally grateful to have been in their family. I have literally received healing at their hands.

It is impossible to describe even the smallest bit of the healing acts of my parents. From my birth, my mother has exerted so much of herself to care for me, and the recent bout with cancer was no exception. Day after day, for months, my mother and father cared for me and helped me to heal. I didn't show them nearly the appreciation they deserved for all the time and effort they sacrificed for me, but I feel it engraved permanently on my heart.

It is through giving thanks for these expressions of love that part of my heart was able to heal. The many people who surrounded, lifted, and served me are a living example of the words in Mosiah 18. My family, friends, and ward members were "willing to bear [my] burdens, that they may be light; yea, and [were] willing to mourn with [me]; yea, and comfort [me when I stood] in need of comfort" (Mosiah 18:8–9). I was truly comforted by my friends and family who were so willing to serve me. My burdens were lifted because of their Christlike charity. They ministered to me, and they brought healing into my life.

But much of my healing took a long, long time. In fact, in many ways, I am still healing from all I experienced. So much damage had been done, and my wounds and hurt ran deep. My healing was truly a day-by-day, minute-by-minute, second-by-second experience. It took months for my body to regain strength. I was always in pain, but with time it decreased. I worked hard to return my body to health, and trying to remain patient and not discouraged was an incredible challenge.

Do you, like me, have a deep desire to receive healing

in your life? Perhaps you have even wished for a helicopter to lift you from the middle of a painful trial. At times it does not seem conceivable, but I know that healing will come. Much healing is available in this life, made possible through the mercies of Jesus Christ, our own diligence and repentance, and the love of others.

However, total and complete healing will come only in the resurrection. I don't understand exactly how it will work, but I know that it will. Through the Atonement of Christ, you and I will receive perfected bodies, and all the hurts and pains of this life will be made right.

I know that all my struggles through the afflictions of mortality will be worth it if I remain faithful to the Savior. In this life and in the next, Christ is my holy place of healing.

Chapter Eight

THE ENABLING POWER

When I was a little girl, I had great adventures as a superhero in my own kingdom. I grew up in a beautiful valley in northern California, where green hills dotted with oak trees framed the valley floor. In the spring, gorgeous grape vineyards sprang from the chocolate soil. The carpet of green would soon appear, followed by vibrant, mustard-yellow flowers. The almond trees with their bright pink blossoms stood as sentries. This was my kingdom. I would climb to the top of the hill on which I lived to marvel at its beauty. I sat on the ground and surveyed the land. I was not only the superhero, but the queen as well. After I had thought of how lucky I was to rule over such an enchanted place, I would stand up, run as fast as I could down the steep slope, flap my arms, and jump into the air. For just a few seconds, I could fly. I felt like Superman. I would then shoot webs from my wrists, Spider-man-style, and make it the rest of the way home swinging from cherry tree to cherry tree. The "bad guys" had no chance in my kingdom since I had powers and could stop them dead in their tracks. After all, I had my webs and my magic lasso. If occasion demanded, I also could jump, see, and hear like the bionic man and woman.

Call it imagination, or perhaps delusion, but as a little girl I needed strength to overcome great challenges and power beyond my own. I longed for a place that was free from trouble where I could feel peace, comfort, and safety.

Now that I am older, I still long for such a place. Through my "grown-up" trials, I have wished to have more strength and power than I possess. Sometimes the load I carry is just too heavy for me.

In the course of the numerous physical trials I have experienced, many people have asked, "Kris, how do you do it?" I have always answered that it is only Christ's help that gets me through. That is the complete truth. I wouldn't be able to do much of anything without the grace of Christ, made possible through His Atonement. But sometimes I forget that I don't have to carry the burden alone.

When I lost my sight, well-meaning people would comment, "You can do it, Kris. Heavenly Father wouldn't give you anything you couldn't handle." Although that was meant as encouragement, it made me feel horrible. I already felt powerless, weak, and unable to cope with my new life. Those words just drove the knife in further. I would cry inside, "I really *can't* handle this! I have no more strength left. Everyone thinks I am so brave when I am scared to death!"

It was then that truth given through the Holy Ghost entered my mind and heart. The idea that I wouldn't be given anything I couldn't handle was not true! If it were, then there would be no need for Christ. I had been given many things to handle that required more power than I had. Only when I accessed the power of Jesus Christ would my strength be magnified and my weaknesses overcome.

This tutoring from the Spirit has become a holy place and has changed my outlook. Whenever I am faced with an extreme difficulty, I remind myself that I can do it *through the grace of my Savior.* Now, when someone says,

"Heavenly Father won't give you anything you can't handle," I add, "with Christ's help."

I love the description of the word *grace* in the Bible Dictionary. Grace is described as a "divine means of help or strength" and "an enabling power." Additionally, through the grace of Christ, made possible by His Atonement, you and I will be raised to a state of immortality, and through our faithfulness and His grace we can receive eternal life. However, it is Christ's daily gift of grace that I wish to discuss.

Although I do pretty well functioning in my life in the dark, every so often I get discouraged. I call these times my "hard blind days." If my husband asks how I am doing and I reply, "It's a hard blind day," he knows what I mean. I am, again, feeling sad that I had to go through the whole cancer-and-blindness ordeal. I am tired of my limitations and physical pain. Once more, I am frustrated because I hurt myself so often, like when someone leaves the dishwasher door open and I bruise my shins for the millionth time. On my "hard blind days," I think of all the things I wish I could do that I can't. I wish I could read a book to my boys or drive them somewhere—anywhere. So many things would be easier if I could just see, but, sadly, that will never happen in this life.

During these days of sadness and discouragement, I need my superpowers to keep me going. Unfortunately, my Underoos don't fit anymore, I don't dare to put on blue tights, and I'd probably trip over my cape if I had one. But, seriously, there is a super power that I can access when I need extra strength. As I give my best effort, I can receive Christ's "enabling power." In prayer, I ask for the gift of grace to help me do the things that are required of me but that I don't have the power to accomplish. Then I get up and get to work.

Christ's grace, the "divine means of help or strength," is available to all of us as we exercise faith in the Savior and repent of our sins. It can help us accomplish good things that we wouldn't be able to do on our own.

In the aftermath of all my surgeries, I still had some unfinished business to take care of: the absence of my right eye. Fixing this problem was something I didn't have the strength to deal with. After all, there was no satisfactory fix. It was going to take more power to handle this situation than I possessed.

When I found out my options for camouflaging the

mess that had been created of my face, I was frantic with desperation. A black patch strung around my head, or glasses with an attached eyeball? There was no way I could live my life as a pirate or Mrs. Potato Head! Neither option would do. I couldn't conceive of living in such a way.

After two more operations and more facial rearranging and recovery, it was time to face the problem. I did some investigating and found that there was a type of prosthetic, made from silicone, that could be designed for me. It didn't sound appealing, but it was better than the pirate patch.

I went through the process of having molds made of my face, and the silicone colored to match my skin. Inside the silicone, which would act as my eyelids, would sit an artificial eyeball. The whole prosthetic would be held to my skin with adhesive.

But that's not all. I would then need to wear glasses to camouflage the edge of the prosthetic so it wasn't as obvious. I thought that was the dumbest thing I had ever heard. Glasses had never been able to help me through all my years of limited vision, and now that I was blind, I would have to wear them?

It was all more than I could take. I feared I would look

like a monster, and I prayed for heavenly help nearly every second of the experience. I remember the first time my four-year-old saw me wearing the new prosthetic.

"You look weird, Mommy!" was his reaction.

Needless to say, I wept. The unfairness of all I had to go through hit me yet again. I was grateful that my life had been preserved, but that life was now being swamped with difficulties beyond my imagination. I didn't think I could actually go out in public with my new face.

However, I was given strength to go forward, and soon I was able to handle it more easily. It is difficult every morning to have to glue on my eye. It feels uncomfortable and unnatural, but that is my reality. Each day, when it's time to adhere the prosthetic, I have a moment when I think, "I can't believe I have to do this!"

I am trying now to use that feeling as a reminder to pray for the gift of grace. I pray that I will have the physical and emotional strength to do whatever lies before me each day, no matter how hard. If I constantly turn to my Savior, I know He will always be there to add His strength to what little strength I possess.

You don't, however, have to be missing body parts to access Christ's "enabling power." Through His Atonement,

His grace is available to all who exercise faith in Him and repent of sin. You and I do not have to lift our burdens alone. In fact, we should not. Christ performed the miraculous Atonement to assist all of us. When we do not plead for the grace of Christ to assist us, we only hurt ourselves and miss out on what could be a holy place.

I encourage you to seek the gift of grace. Christ will give you power to do the things in your life that seem beyond your capacity. Turn to Him for the help you need, and He will give you His "divine means of help." Throughout my life, He has been my source of power and strength. He is my holy place of grace.

Chapter Nine

LIGHT FROM THE SON

When I first became blind, the thing I wanted most was light. I craved it. I ached for it. It seemed that my body, mind, and spirit longed for even the smallest glimmer of the light that I had enjoyed my whole life but that now was denied me. I literally went through withdrawals. Out of habit, when I went into a room, I would flip on the light switch and expect to see; however, it never worked. I felt the sunshine on my face when I went outside, but for me it was darker than midnight.

I wished for a way to leave the endless night. Sleep was my only escape. In my dreams, I could see. There were bright, vivid colors, and I could return to the world that had been taken away from me. Also, the intense physical pain did not plague me in my sleep. I only wished I did not have to wake up. But day always came, and so did my reality of blackness and pain. Many mornings, I still wake up disappointed at the darkness that encompasses me. I wish I could crawl back under the covers to my lost world of light and stay there.

I also experienced many foreign sensations and feelings after losing my vision. Since my brain knew what it was like to see, it created illusions that seemed real. I could "see" outlines of objects around my house, my shadowy reflection in the mirror, and phantom light. It was so strange to me. There was no way that my brain could access light from the outside world, yet it manufactured it somehow.

I had heard about people who had had their limbs amputated, yet they could feel pain or itching sensations where their limbs had been. That "phantom pain" is now a little more understandable to me. The lights and colors I saw were, of course, not real, but oddly comforting. It was as though my mind longed for light like I did, and if it wasn't going to get any, it would create it.

Bright, fluorescent yellows and greens would fill my former field of vision. Sometimes a small, glowing white light would appear and then grow until it filled my view. I held onto this welcomed fiction and was saddened when it faded.

I still see light in my mind, but it has changed from the bright colors to a fuzzy image of white. It's kind of like when the picture doesn't come in on the television and the blurry dots of light flicker on the screen. Yet I am glad for it. At times, I'll comment, "Man, is it dark in here!" People think I've lost my mind. My son will say, "Mom, it's 'cause you're blind." (Like I could forget.) Usually, I comment on the darkness when I have no phantom lights to see. Even though it isn't real, the absence of my phantom light makes my black world darker. I get quite excited when I see a flash of blue or red. It sure livens things up.

However, my phantom light is false light. It doesn't keep me from walking into walls or tripping over shoes left in the middle of the floor. I can't rely on it to show me my way. Only true, real light can do that.

I learned a powerful lesson about light during the Christmas season of 2004. That season marked one full year since I had entered my "Dark Ages." It was incredibly difficult, and I missed seeing all the festive decorations and bright lights. I longed to see a Christmas tree covered in lights and topped with a bright star. It didn't seem like the holidays without the sight of the multicolored house lights around town, and I couldn't get into the spirit of things.

Then, an idea hit me. The Holy Ghost reminded me that Christ is the true Light. I was not denied access to His brightness. Even though I couldn't see the illuminated decorations, I could feel heaven's true Light.

Each time I became sad because I couldn't see the Christmas lights, I remembered Christ by thinking of the attributes He possessed that began with each letter of the word *light*. Christ became my Christmas Light.

L—Love. I thought about Jesus Christ being a God of love. Christmas was a time to celebrate the love the Father had in giving His Son to the world and to me. Christ demonstrated His immense love when He performed the Atonement. His boundless love has seen me through so much darkness.

I—Intelligence. Christ is also a God of intelligence. He knows the beginning from the end and how I fit into that picture. His knowledge and wisdom will never fail, and I can place my trust in Him.

G—Grace. The grace of Christ, made possible through His Atonement, gives me the strength to do things beyond my capacity. He offers it to me as I exert all my effort.

There would be no way I could have made it through so much without His gift of grace.

H—Healing. The healing power of my Savior is incomprehensible to me. I realize that He has healed me in so many ways and that there are even more times of healing of which I am unaware.

T—Truth. Christ is a God of truth and cannot lie. I can rely on Him as my source of truth and knowledge.

Every time I became discouraged and longed for light, I rehearsed those attributes in my mind. That exercise got me into the Christmas spirit, but, more important, it got the spirit into me. Instead of that Christmas being sad and dark, it became a holy place where I felt the Light.

As I tried to come to terms with my new realities and limitations, I searched for comfort and counsel in the scriptures. I missed being able to actually read the words with my eyes, but was grateful for my ability to listen to my Book of Mormon recordings on tape. I remember coming across a single verse from Abinadi's words to the wicked priests of King Noah, and its message of Christ struck me: "He is the light and the life of the world; yea, a light that is endless, that can never be darkened; yea, and also a life

which is endless, that there can be no more death"
(Mosiah 16:9).

The two things that I had worried over and fought to
maintain the past year were light and life. I had barely held
onto my life, and I had lost the battle for light. However,
Christ *is* and *provides* both. His light will never be extinguished. It is "endless." Even though I have lost my ability
to see light in this life, I can still remain faithful and see
the Light in the next. His divine life is eternal, and death
cannot harm Him again. Through Him I can be resur-
rected and be freed from death's grasp. My life, too, will
become endless. Again, Christ is the answer. He is the holy
place of light and life.

I had many opportunities to remember my Savior and
His light as I adjusted to my blindness. A few months after
my last brain surgery, when my health would permit, I
began taking classes at the Center for the Blind in Salt
Lake City. Each day for four months I boarded the "short
bus" (our name for the paratransit service I took) and traveled an hour from my home to a training and adjustment
program for the blind and visually impaired. I took courses
to help me function safely and successfully in my life. I
slowly began to decipher Braille and learned how to use

adaptive computers with screen readers. I was taught techniques to help with cooking and cleaning, as well as other activities of daily living. I even learned to knit.

One of the most valuable skills I learned at the Center for the Blind was cane travel. In my mobility and orientation class, I worked one-on-one with an instructor. He taught me the basics of how to use a white cane while walking. First he taught me how to orient myself in a new room. Then we worked in hallways and around the inside of the building. I learned to navigate stairs, and then we moved to the outdoors. My instructor taught me how to travel along sidewalks and how to cross calm streets. The next level of difficulty came when I began crossing the wide, busy streets of downtown Salt Lake City.

It took a tremendous amount of concentration and courage to master the techniques I was being taught. It was terrifying to step out into a busy street on my own, without seeing a thing.

My teacher always walked about fifteen feet behind me to ensure I was safe and to evaluate my progress with each lesson. It was quite unnerving to be followed around by some man I barely knew, but I tried to focus on what was ahead of me instead of wondering if I was doing it right.

Because I was still recovering from many months of illness, emotional trauma, and surgeries, I was often fatigued and weak. I had to force myself to continue placing one foot in front of the other as I stepped into the dark (pun intended).

While I maneuvered my way through each mobility class, I gave myself little pep talks and tried not to give up. With each step, I reminded myself to keep my head and my spirits up. If I kept my head up and my focus forward instead of down, I walked a straighter course. If I hesitated in fear and concentrated on my feet, I drifted and stumbled.

During my mobility walks, I spent a lot of time thinking of Jesus Christ. I was grateful that my Savior, as my Shepherd, had walked the path before me. I clung to the fact that He now traveled the road beside me as my guide.

This was different from my mobility trainer, who watched from a distance and pointed out all my mistakes. Of course, I was thankful for all my trainer taught me. He gave me knowledge I desperately needed to function in my new life. We actually became friends and had fun on our mobility adventures together.

During one lesson, toward the end of the course, we

had a humorous incident that I still laugh about. My trainer had given me the route I was to take and the place we would meet. I was to cross a particular street in downtown Salt Lake that was very busy. After crossing, I was to go east and turn left at the second sidewalk. From there I would walk between two buildings until I came to a grocery store. My instructor was to meet me inside at the customer service desk.

I memorized the route and stepped out into the street.

I have a tendency to veer to the left when I cane, and I must have been doing this as I crossed in the crosswalk. All of a sudden, as I neared the other side of the road, a kind Hispanic woman grabbed my arm, pulled me up onto the sidewalk, and chattered, very concerned, in Spanish. I didn't understand her, but I could tell she was worried about me crossing the street by myself. I smiled, said "Gracias," and continued on my way. I found the second sidewalk and turned left. When I turned into the grocery store, I again heard the woman's animated voice, but this time she sounded upset.

At the customer service desk, I met my teacher as planned. We were soon joined by the store manager, a security guard, and the very agitated Hispanic woman. I soon understood what was happening. I had walked my assigned route across the street, down the sidewalk, through the alley, and into the store. My mobility instructor had followed me at a distance, matching my movements through the course. The kind woman had joined our parade, thinking the suspicious man intended malice toward me, the "blind lady." She was now reporting my trainer as a creepy man who meant me harm.

Calmly, I explained the situation to the security guard and assured him that, although this man might look like a creepy stalker, he was really my mobility instructor. I turned to my teacher and informed him that he was lucky. His fate was in my hands. If he had corrected me during our lesson that day, he would have ended up in the slammer.

Even though I worked hard and made a lot of progress under his tutelage, I couldn't help but compare my mobility trainer's teaching approach to that of my spiritual trainer. Christ beckons me forward and walks beside me. When I stumble, He lifts me and gives me power to continue on. He does more than just watch and correct; He loves. I trust Him as my omniscient guide.

During some lessons, my trainer would take me to the

neighborhood where we had been working, and he would drop me off without disclosing the name of the street I was on. He would give me the coordinates of the place we were to meet, and I was left alone to discover my location and find my way. Yes, I was scared, but I tried to remember the things I had learned. First, I noticed where I was positioned in reference to the sun. If it was morning, and I felt the warmth of the sun on my right, I knew I was facing north. I used the sun as my constant reference. The sun's warmth was my compass. Of course, this got a bit tricky on cloudy days, but then other skills came into play. I depended tremendously on my hearing, and I listened for the sounds of traffic. I gathered information from everything around me to determine where I was.

This, too, turned into a Sunday School lesson for me as I walked and worked. I can tell a lot about my spiritual position as I evaluate how far I am from the Son. If He seems far from me, I know I need to make some adjustments and change my course to better feel His warmth. Listening to the Spirit also keeps me on the right path and close to the Son, my constant reference. Someday, if I use the tools and knowledge I have been given, I will meet my Savior at the end of my journey. There is so much in front of me that is unknown, but the Son is there to guide me with His warmth.

Thinking of Christ helped me turn my discouragement into determination. Instead of staying frustrated with my situation and the difficulty of learning these new techniques, I tried to build my faith. In this way, my many hours of training became another holy place.

When you and I face dark times, how can we access Christ's light to brighten our way? We might minimize the sources of light because of their simplicity, but basic spiritual habits will bring light. I have often been given bits of light as I have pled in prayer and then turned to the scriptures. True doctrine is light, and many times the light of Christ's doctrine, found in the holy scriptures, has illuminated my days of dark sorrow and discouragement. Darkness has fled as I have gained inspiration and light from my patriarchal blessing, worshiped in the temple, and listened to the teachings of the living prophet and the promptings of the Holy Ghost.

I invite you to join me in considering your current position. Whatever problem you are struggling through, where are you in reference to the Son? Can you feel His warmth in your life? What changes do you need to make in your course to bring you closer to His light? Depending on our own light is not enough to get us to our meeting place with the Savior. If we follow it, His true light will lead you and me through darkness toward our journey's end.

With the light of our Savior, we do not walk in darkness. Christ explains this himself in John 8:12: "I am the light of the world: he that followeth me shall not walk in darkness, but shall have the light of life." What a fantastic promise! Christ will light our way through whatever darkness we face, if we follow Him.

I know a little about walking in physical darkness, and I can think of many things I'd rather do. I get extremely tired of the dark. So many things would be easier if I could just see—if I just had access to light. However, spiritual light is so much more important. Spiritual illumination is vital to my progression back to the Father.

I wish I craved the light of the Son as much and as frequently as I do the light from the sun. Perhaps that is why I am given trials. In the times when life is difficult, I realize my need for His light, warmth, and comfort. I am more dependent upon Him for direction and guidance, and I long for the Light. I am grateful for the comfort and warmth, as well as the light I have received from my Savior. He is my holy place of light.

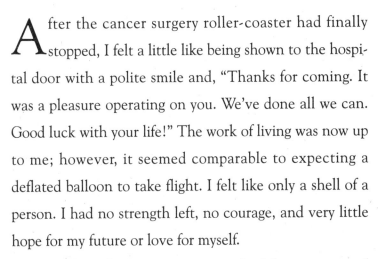

Chapter Ten

FINDING MYSELF THROUGH LAUGHTER

After the cancer surgery roller-coaster had finally stopped, I felt a little like being shown to the hospital door with a polite smile and, "Thanks for coming. It was a pleasure operating on you. We've done all we can. Good luck with your life!" The work of living was now up to me; however, it seemed comparable to expecting a deflated balloon to take flight. I felt like only a shell of a person. I had no strength left, no courage, and very little hope for my future or love for myself.

Each day, after many, many months, life got more and more bearable. Instead of remaining and wallowing in despair, I tried to turn to Christ for hope and happiness.

Now, anyone who was around me during those terrifying and painful months can testify that I was often angry, upset, frustrated, and discouraged. I'm sure they didn't see much hope in my face or in my attitude. I did not blame God for what was happening, but I was miserable and angry at my situation. It was a long process of suffering and pain. So many traumas had crashed down on me that I began, instinctively, to live on the defensive. I felt more like a caged, wounded animal than a human, and I lived on edge and braced for trouble.

Amazingly, about a year following my surgery stint, I began to pull out of the deep, dark sadness that had engulfed me. It was still dark, but I wasn't quite so devastated. I had wondered if I would ever return to the person I was before the cancer and blindness, and I came to realize that the answer was a big, fat "No!" That person was forever changed. I was different physically and emotionally, and that difference could not be erased with time. Time, however, did remove the fear and the pain, and I was able to become accustomed to my limitations and abilities.

Gradually, I found myself—my new self. I was even able to laugh again. Underneath all my hurt, I discovered my long-lost sense of humor. Soon, I realized that my life didn't have to be so solemn and serious all the time. I was able to see that blindness brought with it many humorous situations and conversations.

Being blind feels a whole lot like living with the lens cap on. I run into a lot of things and make a lot of embarrassing mistakes, but these times can be very funny.

One Sunday at church, a woman asked me, "Kris, have you taught your boys sign language yet?"

I couldn't believe she was serious, so I played along.

"No. Why?"

"So you can communicate."

She was serious. I was so glad another lady said something so I didn't burst out with, "Are you nuts?"

"She's blind, not deaf!" was my friend's correction.

I have had other people speak loudly or slowly to me, all because I can't see. Go figure.

Sometimes, when I am out to dinner with my husband, the server will ask him, "What would 'she' like to drink?" (I guess it stands to reason that if I can't see, then I can't hear or think for myself.) I usually respond with, "'She' would like a Sprite and 'he' will have a root beer." I'm not very good at playing helpless.

Recently, I spoke to a group of students at a local school about my blindness. I told them some funny situations and explained that, with a little common sense, many of their questions could be answered. When it was time for "questions and answers" a young girl asked, sincerely confused, "Well, how do you drive?"

I didn't miss a beat. "I stick my white cane out the window and move it back and forth really quickly. If it hits something, I know I need to slow down or drive around it."

The older boys on the back row thought that was pretty funny, but I think the little girl still thinks I can drive. Actually, I explained that I was only joking and the streets were safe from drivers who couldn't see. I have never had a license or driven—at least not legally.

A few years ago, I traveled alone on an airplane and learned firsthand how cattle must feel. Well, maybe it was more like how furniture would feel if furniture could feel. When the plane landed, I explained to the flight attendant that I would need someone to walk to the baggage claim area with me. She asked me to wait until the other passengers had disembarked, and said that someone would be happy to assist me. Well, when everyone had gotten off the plane, I stood up and was led down the skinny aisle to the front. There, the whole crew met me. The captain took my hand and, speaking a bit loudly for my benefit, he introduced himself. Then, he held onto both of my arms, backed me up out of the plane, and sat me down in a waiting wheelchair. I felt like I needed a reverse signal.

Before I knew it, I was whisked off through the little tunnel thing into the airport while the plane's crew called their good-byes behind me. The person pushing the chair didn't speak for a while, and when I told him/her I was able to walk, I deduced my "helper" was a woman. She only said, in an Asian accent, "No. No." Even though I was at least twice her size, she pushed me up and down the inclines of the airport to the baggage claim area. Wow, was she strong! I made it to the baggage carousel in record time. I guess that was the way to go, even though my pride was a bit bent.

Last year, on our family vacation, we stayed overnight in a small Nevada town. While we played in the motel pool, my oldest son and I had a race under water. When I reached the finish line, I realized that I was missing something. Somewhere in the water, I had lost my eye prosthesis. The adhesive had not held it on firmly enough and I panicked in humiliation. Thank heaven no one else was at the pool. My family and I laughed as we played a new family game: "I spy my little eye."

I don't like calling attention to my disability, but walking around with a long white cane makes it inevitable. This journal entry sums up the day I felt like the ward spectacle:

"This past Sunday, James and I were asked to say the prayers in sacrament meeting. I love to pray, but now that I am blind, praying in public gets a bit more difficult than before. We usually sit near the front so that I don't have a long way to cane while everyone watches me go to the podium. After I have said the prayer in the past, I have had a lot of people pat me on the shoulder and sweetly tell me what a wonderful job I do and how brave I am. While I try to be a good sport about the compliments, it is a bit much for just saying a prayer.

"Well, this week we kicked the embarrassment level up a notch. I was all prepared to cane my way up to the stand with a smile on my face. We were positioned on the second row so I wouldn't have far to go. Now, you may be asking why James doesn't just walk me up there. If he does, then we have Benji crying because he wants to come, and Christopher who follows because he doesn't want to be left alone. So instead of making it a family affair, I find it just as simple to get myself up to the podium. Well, when the meeting was over, the counselor conducting, said, 'We'll now close with a closing prayer by Sister Belcher. We've asked one of our deacons to walk Kris up here.' Well, that was news to me. Just then, I felt someone sit down by me on the pew. It was my assigned deacon guide dog. I swallowed my glee (pride) and took his arm to go to the front. He did pretty well guiding me. That is, he did pretty well up until the point where he said, 'Here is the podium,' and walked away. So I took a step toward the audience and there was no podium. He had left me several feet from it. The bishop thought I was going to fall over the edge of the rostrum and sent both counselors to help save me. They each grabbed an arm—not very softly, I might add—and did a kind of shuffle step sideways. 'Here's the podium. No, wait. Yep, there you go,' was the whispered dialogue. By that time I was ready to scream! But I remained calm and just smiled as I stood there collecting myself enough to pray. Wow! Who knew church could be so entertaining? I knew that everyone was just trying to help (even though I didn't ask for it). I worked at being gracious and then tried for the next two hours to stop shaking my head in disbelief.

"Next time I am asked to pray in sacrament meeting,

I'm going to have my little deacon guide dog just bring me a roving microphone! Amen."

Although I can laugh about these experiences, blindness really isn't funny. There are days when I wish I could rip off the darn lens cap. However, now that I can laugh again, I find that it makes this trial, and others, easier to endure. When I find reasons to laugh, I am not stuck in despair or sorrow, and I am free to look for holy places even when my life is difficult and filled with the challenges of mortality.

Laughter has helped me to relax and not be on the defense around other people. It has also put others, as well as myself, more at ease with my blindness. By washing away some of my fears and frustrations, laughter has also aided in my discovery of another holy place. That holy place is me. I finally got to a point where I liked myself again. Sure, my body and emotions were badly damaged, but I am all right. With the power of my Savior, I have come through this devastating experience as well as past difficulties. I didn't think I could live a happy life blind, but I am doing it!

Our spirits are incredible! They are holy—holy because they come directly from Heavenly Father. I know that He loves each of us for who we are—not just who we are on the outside, but who we really are on the inside. That is not just a nice little thing we say to make those who are less than beautiful feel good. It is really true. You and I are loved completely and absolutely by our Heavenly Father.

I know that my spirit is holy. When I keep this in mind, I am not so hard on myself. I can laugh amid the struggle. Contrary to my previous thoughts, I can even be happy. Underneath the sorrow and pain, I have found someone worthwhile, someone wonderful, someone holy.

Chapter Eleven

LIVING WITH HOPE

Unfortunately, not every difficulty can be resolved or wrapped up nicely, ready to submit to a Church magazine. Not every baby comes home from the hospital; disease is not always cured; death is not always escaped; tragedies and broken hearts cannot always be avoided. Not every story in life has a happy ending. Oftentimes, despair seems to suffocate hope as trials and hardships continue their barrage.

Many people have commented that I have had my share of trials and someone else's share as well. I have laughed and responded, "Well, I just want to get my money's worth out of mortality."

Somehow, we think that there ought to be a level of suffering where, once we reach it, we shouldn't have to suffer anymore. That sounds good, but that isn't the plan we supported in the premortal world. Mortality—all of it—is designed to try our faith and to help us grow to be more like our Heavenly Father. The earthly trials don't, and won't, stop until death.

After I crumbled from the cancer and blindness, I hoped that I would get a break from physical problems for a little while. However, that was not the case. Once again I got a helicopter ride, but this time it didn't lift me out of my troubles. It took me to the intensive care unit at LDS Hospital in Salt Lake City.

Early one morning in May 2006, my husband noticed that I was acting as if I were in pain while I was asleep. He woke up a while later and found that I had fallen out of bed and was wedged between the bed and my nightstand. I was moaning and flailing around. This would have been funny, but when he pulled me out, he saw that I was unconscious. He called a neighbor, a former EMT, who rushed right over to help. James then called 911, and the adventure began.

The ambulance delivered me to the hospital nearby, and then I was transferred via Life Flight to Salt Lake. My body had gone into septic shock due to a severe case of spinal meningitis, and the doctors and nurses worked to stabilize my condition. However, there was not much hope for my survival. If I did live, it was probable that I would have severe brain damage.

When James reached the hospital, he was greeted by a doctor with, "I hope you are prepared for your wife to be a vegetable."

I remained in a coma-like state for four days. Miraculously, I awoke. Still, my prognosis was not good.

Again, many people fasted and prayed on my behalf. I began pulling out of danger, and there was no apparent brain damage.

After two weeks in the hospital, I was released to go home. The doctors were flabbergasted. There was no plausible reason for my recovery. I logically should have died or had brain damage. However, I knew that, once again, I had been preserved and protected by the power of God. This was the second time I had suffered from spinal meningitis, and in both cases Heavenly Father had healed me and I was spared any serious side effects.

My recovery was long and horrendously painful, but I was alive. Each day, I was cared for by the sweet sisters in the Relief Society in my new ward. They and my extended family took care of my children, my home, and everything else that was needed. Again, I was amazed by and grateful for the love and kindness of those around me.

Many times, when I have endured something difficult, I worry about what might be coming next, or what I am going to be asked to suffer through tomorrow. It can be so natural to fear the future and the "what-ifs."

But we don't have to live in fear or dread; there is a better way.

That better way is to live in hope—hope in Jesus Christ. I cling to the promise found in Ether 12:4: "Wherefore, whoso believeth in God might with surety hope for a better world, yea, even a place at the right hand of God, which hope cometh of faith, maketh an anchor to the souls of men, which would make them sure and stead-fast, always abounding in good works, being led to glorify God."

That verse of scripture is a holy place for me. During many long, miserable hours of recovery, I have recited it over and over in my mind. Thinking of "a better world" has helped me wade through the hardships in this world. Mortality has its perks, but it sure can hurt. Throughout my suffering, I longed for a better world. I have tried to remember that, through Christ, I can one day live in a world free of suffering, pain, blindness, sadness, and trial. I do believe in God, and I long for the place at His right hand where my suffering will be over.

But we don't have to wait for the next life for things to be better. I have found that hope in Jesus Christ brings me peace. With that peace, I am able to live a life of faith instead of fear, a life of happiness instead of hopelessness. Peace and hope don't take away the pain, nor do they minimize our trials. But remembering that there is "a better world" and hoping for it has helped me take one more step forward through difficulties when I didn't think it was possible.

My future, like yours, is uncertain. With the body I have been given, it is more than likely that I will continue to have health problems. I will always be at risk for additional cancer, and, who knows, my airhead condition may return. Yes, this scares me. I don't want to hurt anymore. However, I can't dwell on what might happen. If I did, I would be paralyzed with fear.

My husband tells me that I am not allowed to have any more life-threatening illnesses. The next time something happens to me, he says he won't call 911; he'll just call the home teachers, and they'll have to deal with it. I'm sure glad we have great home teachers!

Actually, James and I joke like this because we know that our trials are not over. We try to change the things we have control over and leave the future in the Lord's hands. It is easier said than done, but it is part of how we try to live with hope.

Hope also gives me courage. When I served as a missionary in the Kentucky Louisville Mission, I experienced many days of discouragement. I found that these words of the Prophet Joseph Smith energized me and gave me courage to keep going, even when the days were long and difficult: "Brethren, shall we not go on in so great a cause? Go forward and not backward. Courage, brethren; and on, on to the victory! Let your hearts rejoice, and be exceedingly glad" (D&C 128:22).

Since my days as a missionary, I have applied this scripture to many other situations. During trials and afflictions, although it is challenging, it is worth it to "go forward and not backward."

When we live with hope, we can have courage to continue through the hard times that will come. Our lives of hope will allow our hearts to rejoice, and we can go forward, "on to the victory" (D&C 128:22)—our victory in "a better world . . . at the right hand of God" (Ether 12:4).

Chapter Twelve

THE HOLY ONE

J esus Christ stands as my perfect example of how to create a holy place. I think of all He suffered. He—the divine Son of God—was mocked, reviled, betrayed, beaten, and crucified. But why did Christ experience such great agony when He possessed power to stop His persecutors?

Our Savior "suffereth it, because of his loving kindness and his long-suffering towards the children of men" (1 Nephi 19:9). Because of His love for you and me, He "suffereth it." That was His mission, part of the sacred Atonement. "And he cometh into the world that he may save all men if they will hearken unto his voice; for behold, he suffereth the pains of all men, yea, the pains of every living creature, both men, women, and children, who belong to the family of Adam. And he suffereth this that the resurrection might pass upon all men, that all might stand before him at the great and judgment day" (2 Nephi 9:21–22).

There was a glorious purpose for Christ's suffering. Part of that purpose was to assist you and me through the difficulties of mortal life. There is nothing we have gone through or will go through that Christ does not understand. He literally suffered in Gethsemane and on Golgotha, and He comprehends our pain and feelings perfectly. He is there, with power, to help us through our own suffering.

I think of Jesus in the Garden of Gethsemane. What agony He willingly endured for us, His brothers and sisters! These sacred words, and His submissive and broken heart, brought holiness to His pain: "O my Father, if it be possible, let this cup pass from me: nevertheless not as I will, but as thou wilt" (Matthew 26:39). The Father's will was more important than His own.

That is how it should be for me. When hard times come, if I seek and obey the Father's will, my pain, hurt, frustrations, worries, and suffering will become holy places.

If I am humble, I will be malleable in His hands, and my holy places will be created in His intended way.

I don't understand all the "whys" of all I have suffered, but I do know that through my trials I have come to know and love my Savior more deeply. Jesus Christ, the Holy One, has brought me through the trials of mortality. I know that He is the literal son of the Eternal Father. He came to earth to prepare a way for us to return to and live with God.

As you have journeyed with me through some of the hard times and holy places of my life, I hope the Spirit has touched your heart. I hope you have found principles that will help you construct holy places out of your struggles. Please know that there is a purpose in your suffering. You and I are being changed, remodeled, stretched, and polished for eternal glory. If we trust in and choose Christ amid our difficulties, our hard times will become holy, and we will be led by Him back to our Father in Heaven.

Looking back, I wish I could have comforted the woman I was five years ago. I wish I could hold her in my arms and promise her, in a way she would believe, that she would make it. The pain, I would explain, will eventually subside. I would tell her that she would smile and even laugh again. Though it seemed inconceivable, I would convince her that life was worth living. I would hold her and allow the sobs to come. Then, I would encourage her to keep praying, keep hoping, and keep trusting as she put one shaky foot in front of the other.

However, the woman I used to be had to struggle. That was part of the trial—I had to build my holy places amid the refining fire.

Gratefully, I was never left to struggle alone. I was comforted by the presence of the Holy Ghost and the love and strength of my Savior and Heavenly Father. I may have lost my sight, but my vision has never been clearer. I now see that each hard time that became a holy place for me brought me once step closer to Jesus Christ—my true holy place.

SHARE YOUR STORY

In this book, I share many of the agonizing struggles I have experienced, and the earthly and heavenly help I have received. Now I invite you to share your story. How have you seen your hard times become holy places in your life? Please do not share personal sins—your own or those of others—but relate those sweet experiences that helped you endure adversity or tragedy. How have difficulties and trials made you stronger? How have you seen the hand of Christ in your life?

Please email me with your experiences at **hardtimes andholyplaces@digis.net**. If you would like to share your experiences with others, I will post them on my blog, **www.hardtimesandholyplaces.blogspot.com**. In this way, I hope we can all be lifted by one another and together create many more holy places.